Praise for *The Emancipation of God*

Newer approaches to biblical interpretation can address the multiple (and sometimes contradictory) biblical traditions, the significance of different communities of readers and their respective histories and contexts, interdisciplinary insights, and the theological implications of our interpretations, among other things. It is a daunting task, but in *The Emancipation of God: Postmarks on Cultural Prophecy,* Walter Brueggemann uses these specific approaches to offer new insights on the Bible and its meaning for a life of faith amid today's seemingly intractable divisions. This book is an important resource that will serve us well.

—Cheryl B. Anderson, professor emerita of Old Testament, Garrett-Evangelical Theological Seminary

This collection is a rare gift for all interpreters and proclaimers of biblical texts for church and culture. Walter Brueggemann continues to be the most significant biblical theologian speaking to church and culture in our day. *The Emancipation of God: Postmarks on Cultural Prophecy* gives us all the revealing opportunity to see him at work; he clearly identifies his method and then illustrates it immediately in the first essay on the debate over the Bible and human sexuality. Brueggemann regularly shows tensions in biblical texts and how he navigates those tensions. In three parts he mingles pieces on the emancipation of God, the church, and the neighborhood. Don't miss this jewel of delightful and remarkably crafted biblical interpretations.

—W. H. Bellinger Jr., professor emeritus of religion, Baylor University; author of *Psalms as a Grammar for Faith* and *Introducing Old Testament Theology*

THE EMANCIPATION OF GOD

THE EMANCIPATION OF GOD

POSTMARKS ON CULTURAL PROPHECY

WALTER BRUEGGEMANN

CONRAD L. KANAGY
Editor

Fortress Press
Minneapolis

THE EMANCIPATION OF GOD
Postmarks on Cultural Prophecy

Library of Congress Control Number: 2023026121 (print)

Cover image: a blurry photo of a tree and a fence by jrkorpa/UnSplash
Cover design: John Lucas

Print ISBN: 978-1-5064-9823-2
eBook ISBN: 978-1-5064-9824-9

CONTENTS

PREFACE

I approached Walter Brueggemann about writing his biography in February 2022. After penning more than one hundred books in the previous six decades, Walter had just begun blogging as his preferred way of broadcasting his latest reflections. The fact that he adapted the blog as a platform for communicating illustrates one of the qualities that has kept Brueggemann's voice alive and relevant for so long. The man lives in the present in all its fullness and in all his fullness.

He reads seven to eight books each week and two newspapers daily. A trip to the local library to return last week's haul and to check out another batch is a regular part of a week's activities for Walter, now chauffeured by his wife, Tia. He has an insatiable appetite for knowing what is happening in the world. He always has. Forced to read and reread the thirty books in his high school library, an astute teacher began bringing books for Walter from the local Blackburn, Missouri, library. His pastor father, August, subscribed to *Christian Century* without ever reading it. But Walter did—and perhaps that is why August maintained the subscription. As a seminary professor, Walter's students consistently discovered that he was always the first to read every book the library staff purchased.

The uniqueness of the blog as a communication device is the personal and immediate connection it creates for both author and reader. Rather than writing alone in his Eden Seminary hideaway, imagining that somebody will read that day's words within a year or two, the blogger knows that what they write will be read within minutes of being posted. The blog also creates a less formal space, and bloggers invariably reveal more of their inner selves, opening space for personal relationships between writer and reader.

So just as I began digging into the biographical basement of Walter's nine decades for glimpses of what made the man who he was, serendipitously or by grace, he had already begun opening himself to readers in new ways. The blog posts in this book reveal more about Brueggemann's inner thoughts and daily life than anything he has written to date. Did we know he and Tia enjoyed drives along Lake Michigan, watching the ducks negotiate wind and waves? Did we know that Walter was a cat lover? Could anybody else connect cats and ducks to the biblical text like Walter?

Those who write autobiographies or memoirs know that priming the pump of memory and emotion tends to bring a geyser of a long-forgotten history. By the time I approached Walter for his story, he had already begun pumping. While I would help move the handle up and down for the next five months, the water was already flowing. I simply placed a bucket beneath.

This book and its sister volume—*Real World Faith* (Fortress Press 2023)—are bookends to *Walter Brueggemann's Prophetic Imagination: A Theological Biography*, in a way none of us could have seen in advance. The three volumes together complete the "show and tell" of Walter's formation, his hermeneutical method, and his deeply held beliefs about the biblical text and the God of that text.

During my interviews with Walter, he described that method as a three-step approach. Make the historical, linguistic, and biographical connections within the biblical text, add "sociology" to the mix by examining contemporary events in today's world, and then apply theology by asking what God was doing then that may parallel what God might just be up to now.

The essays in these two volumes surrounding the biography show how Walter has been working this unique method for decades and why the passage of time has not been able to thwart his voice. Most of the essays exhibit the very method that he described to me by reviewing a book or two he just happened to be reading, discussing it in light of the present, and then placing it all under the light of what God was doing in some biblical text and what God may be doing now. We now have a chance to see with enhanced clarity what was in the master prophet's heart and head all along. We get to watch the craftsman at work. And as always, we are brought into the presence of a God whose entire intent and full energies are the emancipation of all creation from the empires and powers that have imposed themselves upon us and dimmed our prophetic imaginations.

Indeed, the blog essays in both volumes emancipate us to see as most real, not the world of such empires and powers, but that alternative reality of God that lies ahead of those who, by faith, long for that "better country."

Conrad L. Kanagy
Elizabethtown, PA

PRAYER

Fresh from the Word

(On reading Isaiah 55:10–13)

At the outset there was the silence of despair.
And then You spoke:
You said, "Let there be light."
You said, "Let my people go."
You said, "Comfort, comfort my people."
Your word became flesh before our very eyes:
Light became creation;
Emancipation became covenant people;
Comfort became homecoming.
Your word is not empty, but full of futures.
You said, "Love God" and we are summoned.
You said, "Love neighbor" and we are implicated.
You said "Follow me" and we are on a different way with you.
Your word, in its life-giving power, addresses us every day.
Your word, in its life-dispatching force, empowers us every day.
Your word, in its restorative passion, makes new every day.
We are creatures of your word;
we cannot be otherwise;
we would not choose to be otherwise.
It is because of your faithful word that we are on our way . . .
rejoicing;
on our way in freedom, mercy, compassion, and justice,
on our way to neighborly well-being,
on our way rejoicing. Amen.

Walter Brueggemann
March 26, 2022

INTRODUCTION

All Things Emancipated

This collection of essays represents the second of two "bookend" volumes to the recently released *Walter Brueggemann's Prophetic Imagination: A Theological Biography* (Fortress Press 2023). The first volume is *Real World Faith* (Fortress Press 2023). Both comprise former blog posts written by Brueggemann as the last venue for his rich theological reflections, a platform he calls "just right" for this season of life as he approaches his ninetieth birthday.

These essays allow us to experience the "role exit" of one of history's most significant theologians, who by God's grace has been given time and health to correct, redefine, deny, and affirm what he has written across six decades. Like Baruch for Jeremiah, my task as biographer was to assist and to catch the rich, sweet, and refreshing water pouring forth from the deep well of Walter Brueggemann's life. This task was more manageable on some days than others. But I soon learned that the floodgates opened if I relied on the heuristic devices that he often used in the biblical text. Once he began to encounter his life as a text to be exegeted, we quickly moved into the depths of his biographical basement.

One of the rhetorical devices that Brueggemann has long used is that of the "pivot." He writes about how God pivots, how Jeremiah pivots, and how Israel pivots. When I asked, "Walter, when in your life did you pivot?" he readily acknowledged vital moments when he stopped going one direction to go another. And each instance he recognized as a movement or pivot "from moralism to freedom." Or from conformity to emancipation. From closed categories to open-ended ones. From a neutered God to a God who roamed wild and free.

From a church domesticated by the surrounding culture and status quo to one that broke itself free from chains of tradition and rational structures. From neighborhoods segregated by race, class, and wealth to those where caring for one another regardless of social identity began to reflect the Shalom of God's reign.

The longer that Walter has written, the clearer he has become that the intention of Jesus's life, ministry, and death was to set the captives free—captives from all kinds of enslavement and bondage. And, of course, he sees Jesus as an extension of what YHWH was up to in the Old Testament. As you read the essays of this book, you will see the masterful grasp of this prophet and preacher again upon the entire biblical canon, moving freely across Old and New Testament texts. Somewhere along the line, Brueggemann was providentially emancipated from the historical forms of interpretation he encountered in seminary to a livelier, more buoyant, and more relational understanding of the biblical text. Along the way to finding his own emancipation, he also freed an entire field of biblical interpreters from confinement to a form-critical method that, in his words, was "moribund" and "offered nothing to the church." He called his method interpretive and social scientific but mostly just "post-critical." Whatever one calls it, this new approach was just one of many byproducts resulting from the integration of his personal yearning for and experience of emancipation with the emancipation of his theological and spiritual life. The freer Walter became, the freer became his God. The freer he became, the more he saw the constraints of empire and royal consciousness on the church and the need for its emancipation. The freer he found himself, the more he called for all humanity in local and worldwide neighborhoods to be emancipated from fear of the "other," violence, poverty, greed, and injustice.

While Brueggemann may not have called his approach post-critical as early as the 1960s, he was already well beyond the form-critical approach of his day by that time. The man's early imagination of what God was up to among God's people in the Old Testament biblical text was paired with what God might be up to in God's people today. The reigning scholars of biblical studies avoided these questions as irrelevant, too churchy, and below the rigor and interests of the academy. But for Brueggemann, who began to recognize that the church was his habitat rather than the academy, these were just the right questions! So by 1965, he had already published a little essay for Sunday School teachers in a church periodical (*Church School Worker*), describing the most effective way to write or study or teach the story or biography of biblical characters:

1. Study the historical context to determine the particular crisis of faith.
2. Consider the theological issue as it relates to God.
3. Consider how God intervenes in the event to deal with the crisis.
4. Determine how the person involved is a participant in the purposes of God.

Notice how closely these steps mirror Brueggemann's method nearly six decades later. In Brueggemann's theology, God is always the primary actor. And that God is a free God. "Isn't that what it means to be God?" he once jokingly asked me in reference to a peer theologian who long took issue with Brueggemann's view. And the activity of humanity is always done—both in the biblical text and today—within the context of this God who is at once emancipated and sovereign and who desires that all of creation be free as well. This method also reveals the ongoing dialogical relationship between God and humanity. This free God has bound God's self with a people who continually reject the freedom God offers them and turn instead to gods and idols that destroy, capture, and enslave them. But the story of the gospel is of a free God in search of a people who freely choose to belong to that God. And in the glow of that free God, discover an emancipated church and neighborhood!

I once asked Walter why he still loved the church, given the abuse and injustice his father experienced as a pastor and his own criticism of the church enterprise for sixty years. Why wasn't he bitter? Why did he faithfully attend, even somewhat rigidly, according to family members and former students? Without hesitation, he replied: "Because the church still tells the Story. And wherever you find a church, the neighborhood is being cared for. Churches still tell the Story, even those I have no truck with!" For Brueggemann, the faithfulness of a church depends not on whether it swings left or right but on whether it still "tell[s] the old, old story of Jesus and his love."

This defines Walter Brueggemann's central values nurtured in the German evangelical pietism of his day: creating and sustaining communities of faith, telling the gospel story as articulated in the biblical text, and neighborliness expressed in care for the local community around the church. But Walter will also be the first to acknowledge that the church has so often failed its sacred calling. It has trapped God in socially constructed categories that are truer to the culture and powers of the day than to the inspired biblical text. Doing so has left the church vulnerable to the principalities of a world and empires that have tamed and domesticated the church—thus abandoning its Story of freedom for every captive. And the loss of the Story to the church has meant the loss of care and concern for the neighborhood. Indeed, the church and its neighborhood often barely know that the other exists. And so local communities remain trapped in poverty, despair, injustice, racism, and more. Brueggemann believes that the walls separating the church from the neighborhood and the neighborhood from the church must come down. As the prophet Jeremiah proclaimed, any hope that the people of God receive shalom depends on the extent to which they offer that shalom to their neighbors who also happened to be their enemies. The emancipation of God's people depended on the emancipation of the neighborhood. Care for the neighbor and the church will be cared for also. Offer peace to one's neighbors, and houses of peace will open among the most surprising places. Pagans become friends. The "other" becomes human. The enemy becomes an ally. All are set free. Living and sharing the Story always does this.

Across his ninety years, the central focus on the gospel as emancipation has crystalized for Brueggemann. This companion volume to *Real World Faith* illustrates this crystallization by dividing the book into three parts: The Emancipation of God, The Emancipation of the Church, and The Emancipation of the Neighborhood. Were all three to become realities, the kingdom of God would come in its fullness! The prophetic imagination would finally be realized.

As I read and reread the twenty-five essays in this volume, it seemed to me that the axe with which Walter grinds away at the biblical text has only become sharper and freer in cutting through the false reality that has deadened and disabled and muffled the church. After ninety years, Walter recognizes that he is freer than ever. Freer to speak his mind. Freer to see clearly. Freer from the distractions of everyday life of an earlier season. Brueggemann emancipated! Brueggemann unfettered! Brueggemann gone wild! But no more emancipated or wild than the God he has walked with for so many decades and in whose presence he has lived. We should be grateful for the freedom that this prophet is experiencing and the lack of inhibition he reveals in these essays.

The companion book—*Real World Faith*—was composed of essays assembled into five themes, although Brueggemann admits arbitrarily so. They reflected that the work of biblical interpretation "lives at the interface of faith and life [and] continues to press upon us. It is work that, on the one hand, refuses to settle for any 'final solution' of interpretation that we especially treasure because the Spirit is always unsettling our best conclusion. On the other hand, our ongoing interpretive work, when we have courage and wisdom, may always impinge upon our common life in significant ways that continue to empower and perplex us."

I tried to place within each of the three parts of this volume those essays that most clearly reflected the emancipation of God, the church, or the neighborhood. But it was impossible to do so with any precision given Brueggemann's understanding that interpretation occurs at the "interface of faith and life." This book reveals Brueggemann's recognition that true emancipation occurs at the interface of God, the church, and the neighborhood. The three are inseparable in God's economy. Every one of these twenty-six essays, in some way, embodies all three and reflects the prayer of Brueggemann that we—God, church, and neighborhood—finally be set free. "Free at last. Free at last! Thank God Almighty—free at last!"

The first essay in each part is strategically placed. It represents perhaps better than any of the others the critical theme of emancipation of God, church, or neighborhood. They are classic Brueggemann pieces, taking us where we least expected to go but always getting there through the biblical text. As I have often said over the past year, I know of no one who has a higher view of scripture than Brueggemann. And though you may not like where he ends up, he always does by beginning and ending with the biblical text. The essays in this volume are no exception!

Part I

THE EMANCIPATION OF GOD

1

THE EMANCIPATORY WORK OF INTERPRETATION*

IT IS EASY enough to see at first glance why LGBTQ+ people and those who stand in solidarity with them look askance at the Bible. After all, the two most cited biblical texts on the subject are these from the old purity codes of ancient Israel:

> *You shall not lie with a male as with a woman; it is an abomination.* (Leviticus 18:22)
>
> *If a man lies with a male as with a woman, both of them have committed an abomination; they shall be put to death; their blood is upon them.* (Leviticus 20:13)

There they are! There is no way around them. There is no ambiguity in them. They are, moreover, seconded by another verse that occurs in a list of exclusions from the holy people of God:

> *No one whose testicles are crushed or whose penis is cut off shall be admitted to the assembly of the Lord.* (Deuteronomy 23:1)

This text apparently concerns those willingly becoming eunuchs to serve in foreign courts. These texts will do well for those who want

---

* This exposition was first published by *Outreach: An LGBTQ Catholic Resource* in an article titled "How to Read the Bible on Homosexuality." It is reprinted here with the permission of the editor, James Martin, SJ.

it simple, clear, and clean. They seem, moreover, to be echoed in the famous paragraph of the apostle Paul:

> *They exchanged the glory of the immortal God for images resembling a mortal human being or birds or four-footed animals or reptiles. Therefore God gave them up in the lusts of their hearts to impurity, to the degrading of their bodies among themselves, because they exchanged the truth about God for a lie and worshiped and served the creature rather than the Creator, who is blessed forever! Amen. For this reason God gave them up to degrading passions. Their women exchanged natural intercourse for unnatural, and in the same way also the men, giving up natural intercourse with women, were consumed with passion for one another. Men committed shameless acts with men and received in their own persons the due penalty for their error.* (Romans 1:23–27)

Paul's intention here is not fully clear, but he wants to name the most extreme affront of gentiles before the creator God and takes disordered sexual relations as the ultimate affront. This indictment is not as straightforward as those in the tradition of Leviticus, but it does echo those texts. It is impossible to explain away these texts.

Given these most frequently cited texts (that we may designate as "texts of rigor"), how may we understand the Bible given a cultural circumstance very different from that assumed by and reflected in these old traditions? Start with the awareness that the Bible does not speak with a single voice on any topic. Inspired by God as it is, all sorts of people have a say in the complexity of scripture, and we are under the mandate to listen, as best we can, to all its voices. On the question of gender equity and inclusiveness, consider the following to be set alongside the most frequently cited texts. We may designate these texts as "texts of welcome." Thus, the Bible permits very different voices to speak that seem to contradict those texts cited above. Therefore, the prophetic poetry of Isaiah 56:3–8 has been taken to be an exact refutation of the prohibition of Deuteronomy 23:1:

> *Do not let the foreigner joined to the Lord say,*
> *"The Lord will surely separate me from his people";*
> *and do not let the eunuch say, "I am just a dry tree."*
> *For thus says the Lord:*
> *To the eunuchs who keep my sabbaths,*
> *who choose the things that please me*
> *and hold fast my covenant,*
> *I will give, in my house and within my walls,*
> *a monument and a name better than sons and daughters;*
> *I will give them an everlasting name that shall not be cut off. . .*
> *for my house shall be called a house of prayer for all peoples.*
> *Thus says the Lord God,*
> *who gathers the outcasts of Israel,*
> *I will gather others to them*
> *besides those already gathered.* (Isaiah 56:3–8)

This text issues a grand welcome to those excluded so that all are gathered in by this generous gathering God. The temple is for "all peoples," not just the ones who have kept the purity codes.

Beyond this text, we may notice other texts that are tilted toward the inclusion of all people without asking about their qualifications or measuring up the costs that those in control have articulated. Jesus issues a welcoming summons to all those who are weary and heavy-laden:

> *Come to me, all you that are weary and are carrying heavy burdens, and I will give you rest. Take my yoke upon you, and learn from me; for I am gentle and humble in heart, and you will find rest for your souls. For my yoke is easy, and my burden is light.* (Matthew 11:28–30)

No qualification; no exclusion. Jesus is on the side of those who are "worn out." They may be "worn out" by being lower class people who do all the heavy lifting. Or it may be those who are "worn out" by the heavy demands of Torah, imposed by those who make the Torah filled with judgment and exclusion. Since he mentions his "yoke," he contrasts his simple requirements with the heavy demands that are imposed on the community by teachers of rigor. Jesus's quarrel is not with the Torah, but with Torah interpretation that had become, in his time, excessively demanding and restrictive. The burden of discipleship to Jesus is easy, contrasted to the more rigorous teaching of some of his contemporaries. Indeed they had made the Torah in his time exhausting, specializing in trivialities while disregarding the neighborly accents of justice, mercy, and faithfulness (see Matthew 23:23).

A text in Paul (unlike that of Romans 1!) echoes a baptismal formula in which all are welcome without distinction:

> *There is no longer Jew or Greek,*
> *there is no longer slave or free,*
> *there is no longer male or female;*
> *for all of you are one in Christ.* (Galatians 3:28)

No ethnic distinctions; no class distinctions; no gender distinctions! None of that makes any difference "in Christ," that is, in the church. We are all one, and we all may be one. Paul has become impatient with his friends in the churches in Galatia who have tried to order the church according to the rigors of an exclusionary Torah. In response he issues a welcome that overrides all the distinctions that they may have preferred to make.

Finally, among the texts I will cite is the remarkable narrative of Acts 10. The apostle Peter has raised objections to eating food that according to the purity codes is unclean; thus, he adheres to the rigor of the priestly codes not unlike the ones we have seen in Leviticus. His objection, however, is countered by "a voice" that he takes to be the voice of the Lord. Three times that voice came to Peter amid his vigorous objection:

> *What God has made clean, you must not call profane.*
> (Acts 10:15)

The voice contradicts the old purity codes! From this Peter is able to enter into new associations in the church; he declares:

> *You yourselves know that it is unlawful for Jews to associate with or to visit a Gentile, but God has shown me that I should not call anyone profane or unclean.* (Acts 10:28)

And from this, Peter further deduces:

> *I truly understand that God shows no partiality, but in every nation anyone who fears him and does what is right is acceptable to him.* (Acts 10:34)

This is a remarkable moment in Peter's life and the church's life, for it makes clear that the social ordering governed by Christ is beyond the bounds of the rigors of the old exclusivism.

I take the texts I have cited to be a fair representation of the very different voices that sound in scripture. It is impossible to harmonize the mandates to exclusion in Leviticus 18:22, 20:23, and Deuteronomy 23:1 with the welcome stance of Isaiah 56, Matthew 11:29–20, Galatians 3:28, and Acts 10. Other texts might also be cited, but these are typical and representative. As often happens in scripture we are left with texts in deep tension if not in contradiction with each other. The work of reading the Bible responsibly is the adjudication process of these texts that will not fit together. The reason the Bible seems to speak "in one voice" concerning matters that pertain to LGBTQ+ people is that the loud voices most often cite only one set of texts, to the determined disregard of the texts that offer a counter-position. But our serious reading does not allow such a disregard, so we must have all the texts in our purview.

The process of adjudication of biblical texts that do not readily fit together is the work of interpretation. I have termed it "emancipatory work," and I will hope to show why this is so. Every reading of the Bible—no exceptions—is an act of interpretation. No matter how sure and absolute they may sound, there are no "innocent" or "objective" readings. Everyone is engaged in interpretation, so one must consider how we interpret. In what follows I will identify five learnings I have had concerning interpretation, which I hope will be helpful as we read the Bible responsibly around the crisis of gender identity in our culture.

1. All interpretation *filters the text through the life experience of the interpreter*. The matter is inescapable and cannot be avoided. The result, of course, is that with a little effort, one can prove anything in the Bible. It is beneficial to recognize this filtering process. More specifically, I suggest we identify three layers of personhood that likely operate for us in making interpretation.

First, we read the text according to our *vested interests*. Sometimes we are aware of our vested interests, sometimes not. It is not difficult to see this process at work concerning gender issues in the Bible. Second, beneath our vested interests, we read the Bible through the lens of our *fears*, which are sometimes powerful, even if unacknowledged. Third, beneath our vested interests and worries, I believe we read the Bible through the *hurts* we often keep hidden from others and ourselves.

The defining power of *our vested interests, fears, and hurts makes our reading lens seem* sure and reliable. We pretend that we do not read this way, but having as much self-critical awareness as possible is helpful. The matter is urgent for our adjudication of the texts I have cited. It is not difficult to imagine how a particular set of vested interests, fears, and hurts might lead to embracing the "texts of rigor" that I have cited. Conversely, it is not difficult to see how LGBTQ+ people and their allies operate with different filters and so gravitate to the "texts of welcome."

2. *Context inescapably looms large in interpretation.* There are no texts without contexts, and there are no interpreters without context that positions one to read distinctly. Thus, the purity codes of Leviticus reflect a social context in which a community under intense pressure sought to delineate its membership, purpose, and boundaries. The text from Isaiah 56 has as its context the fierce struggle, upon return from exile, to outline the character and quality of the restored community of Israel. One cannot read Isaiah 56 without referencing the opponents of its position in the more rigorous texts, for example, in Ezekiel. And the texts from Acts and Galatians concern a church coming to terms with the radicality of the graciousness of the gospel, a radicality rooted in Judaism that had implications for the church's rich appropriation of its Jewish inheritance.

Each of us, as an interpreter, has a specific context. But we can say something quite general about our shared interpretive context. Western culture (and our place in it) is at a decisive point wherein we are leaving behind many old, long-established patterns of power and meaning and observing the emergence of new ways of power and purpose. It is not difficult to see our moment as an instance anticipated by the prophetic poet:

> *Do not remember the former things,*
> *or consider the things of old.*
> *I am about to do a new thing;*
> *now it springs forth, do you not perceive it?* (Isaiah 43:18–19)

The "old things" among us have long been organized around white male power with its strong tacit assumption of heterosexuality plus a strong accent on American domination. The new thing emerging among us is a multiethnic, multicultural, multiracial, multi-gendered culture in which old privileges and positions of power are placed in deep jeopardy. We can see how our current political-cultural struggles (down to the local school board!) have to do with resisting what is new and protecting and maintaining what is old or, conversely, welcoming what is new with a ready abandonment of what is old. If this formulation from Isaiah roughly fits our circumstance in Western culture, then we can see that the "texts of welcome" are appropriate to our "new thing," while the "texts of rigor" function as a defense of what is old. In many specific ways, our cultural conflicts—and the decisions we must make—reverberate with the big issue of God's coming newness. In the rhetoric of Jesus, this new arrival may approximate among us the "coming of the kingdom of God," except that the coming kingdom is never fully here but is only "at hand," and we must not overestimate the arrival of newness. It is inescapable that we do our interpretive work in a context generally impacted by and shaped by this struggle for what is old and what is new.

3. Texts do not come at us one at a time, *ad seriatim*, but always *in clusters through a trajectory of interpretation*. Thus, it may be correct to say that our several church "denominations" are critical trajectories of interpretation. Location in such a trajectory is essential because it imposes restraints upon us and invites bold imagination in the context of the trajectory. We do not, for the most part, make our interpretation in a vacuum. Instead, we are "surrounded by a cloud of [nameable] witnesses" present with us as we do our interpretive work.

For now, I worship in a United Methodist congregation, and it is easy enough to see the excellent impact of the interpretive trajectory of Methodism. Rooted mainly in Paul's witness concerning God's grace, the specific Methodist dialect, mediated through Pelagius and then Arminius, evokes an accent on the "good works" of the church community in response to God's goodness. That tradition, of course, passed through and was shaped by the wise, knowing hands of John Wesley, and we may say that at present reflects the general perspective of the

World Council of Churches with its acute accent on social justice. The interpretive work of a member of this congregation is happily and inevitably informed by this lively tradition. It is not different from other interpretive trajectories housed in other denominational settings. We are situated in interpretive trajectories that allow for innovation and continuity. Each trajectory provides its members some guardrails for interpretation so we may not run too far afield. However, that also is a matter of adjudication, quite often a matter of deeply contested adjudication.

4. We are, for now, deeply situated in a "crisis of the other." We face folk quite unlike us, and their presence among us is inescapable. We can no longer live in a homogenous community of culture-related "look-alikes." There are, to be sure, many reasons for this new social reality: global trade, more effortless mobility, electronic communication, and mass migrations among them. Thus, we must come to terms with the "other" who disturbs our reductionist management of life through sameness. We have a relatively simple choice that can refer to *the other* as a *threat*, *rival enemy*, or *competitor*, or we may take the other as a *neighbor*. The facts on the ground are always complex, but the simple human realities with each other are not so complicated.

While the matter is pressing and acute in our time, this is not a new challenge. The Bible provides ongoing evidence about the emergency of coming to terms with the other. Thus, the land settlement in the book of Joshua brought Israel face-to-face with the Canaanites, a confrontation that was mixed and tended toward violence. The struggle to maintain the identity and the "purity" of the holy people of God was always a matter of dispute and contention. In the New Testament, the long, laborious process of coming to terms with "gentiles" was a major preoccupation of the early church and a defining issue among the apostles. We can see in Acts that, over time, the early church was ready to allow non-Jews into the community of faith.

And now, among us, the arrival of many "new peoples" remains a significant challenge. Undoubtedly, the "texts of rigor" and the "texts of welcome" offer different stances in the affirmation or negation of the other. And indeed, among the "not like us" folk are LGBTQ+ people who readily violate the old canons of conformity and sameness. Such individuals are among those who easily qualify as "other," but they are no more and no less a challenge than many other "others" among us. And so the church is always re-deciding about the other, for we know that the "other"—LBGTQ+ people among us—will not go away. Thus, we are required to come to terms with them. The trajectory of the "texts of welcome" is that they are to be seen as neighbors who are welcomed to the community's resources and invited to contribute to the community's common well-being. By no stretch of any imagination can it be the truth of the gospel that such "others" as LGBTQ+ people are unwelcome in the community. In that community, there are no "second-class" citizens. We have had to learn that concerning people of color and concerning women. And now, the time has come to face the same gospel reality about LGBTQ+ people as others are welcomed as first-class citizens in the community of faithfulness and justice. We learn that the other is not an unacceptable danger and that the other is not required to give up "otherness" to belong wholly to the community. We in the community of faith, as in the Old and New Testaments, are always called to respond to the other as a neighbor who belongs with "us," even as "we" belong with and for the "other."

5. The gospel is *not to be confused with or identified with the Bible.* The Bible contains various voices damaging the good news of God's love, mercy, and justice. Thus, "biblicism" is a dangerous threat to the faith of the church because it allows into our thinking claims that are contradictory to the news of the gospel. The gospel, unlike the Bible, is unambiguous about God's deep love for all peoples. And where the Bible contradicts that news, as in the "texts of rigor," these texts are seen as "beyond the pale" of gospel attentiveness.

Because

our interpretation is filtered through our close experience,
our context calls for an embrace of God's newness,
our interpretive trajectory is bent toward justice and mercy,
our faith calls us to the embrace of the other, and
our hope is in the God of the gospel and in no other,

the full acceptance and embrace of LGBTQ+ people follow as a clear mandate of the gospel in our time. Claims to the contrary are contradictions of the gospel's truth on all the counts indicated above.

These several learnings about the interpretive process help us in our growth in faith:

- we are warned about the subjectivity of our interpretive inclinations,
- we are invited in our context to receive and welcome God's newness,
- we can identify our interpretive trajectory as one bent toward justice and mercy,
- we may acknowledge the "other" as a neighbor, and
- we can trust the gospel in its critical stance concerning the Bible.

All these angles of interpretation, taken together, authorize a sign for LGBTQ+ people:

WELCOME!

Welcome to the neighborhood! *Welcome* to the gifts of the community! *Welcome* to the work of the community! Welcome to the continuing emancipatory work of interpretation!

2

SOME DARE CALL IT TREASON*

AS REGIMES GROW in their sense of legitimacy, they may finally arrive at a kind of absolute legitimacy that will tolerate no dissent and allow for no legitimate protest or contrary opinion. Such was the case with the Jerusalem establishment of the throne and temple in ancient Israel. King David had claimed royal power based on the steadfast, unconditional commitment of YHWH, the Lord of the Exodus:

> *I will not take my steadfast love from him, as I took it from Saul, whom I put away from before you. Your house and your kingdom shall be made sure forever before me; your throne shall be established forever.* (2 Samuel 7:15–16; see also Psalm 89:1–37)

King Solomon, after David, had built the Jerusalem temple that celebrated the claim that YHWH was a permanent resident in the temple, and for that reason the assured patron and guarantor of the temple and its royal establishment:

---

* My title alludes to the book *None Dare Call It Treason* (1964) by John Stormer. He wrote the book in the wake of Joseph McCarthy and Barry Goldwater with the intent to expose the "many communists" then in the US government. His title refers to a general "refusal" to recognize the widespread danger that he discerned, a discernment that proved wholly false. I use the title from his phrasing now because of the readiness of some, in the wake of Donald Trump, to label any truth-teller as a "traitor" if such a one butts up against their preferred ideological investment.

The Lord has said that he would dwell in thick darkness.
I have built you an exalted house,
a place for you to dwell in forever. (1 Kings 8:12–13)

The combination of *legitimated royalty* and *temple patronage* assured that the royal regime of Jerusalem could grow in its power, wealth, and legitimacy.

There was no doubt that the old Sinai covenant, through its more contemporary representatives, the prophets, would speak critically concerning such absolutism of royal-priestly power claimed for and in Jerusalem. Thus, the prophetic tradition in ancient Israel commits to an ongoing critique of Jerusalem's absolutism, with its insistent advocacy for an alternative neighborly form of political economy. Such a critical alternative was unwelcome in Jerusalem. Thus, in a summary fashion, it is reported that the prophets repeatedly and incessantly warned about such absolutism:

> *Yet the Lord warned Israel and Judah by every prophet and every seer, saying, "Turn from your evil ways and keep the commandments and statutes, in accordance with all the law that I commanded your ancestors and that I sent to you by my servants the prophets." They would not listen but were stubborn, as their ancestors had been, who did not believe in the Lord their God.* (2 Kings 17:13–14)

Jesus sounds a later reprise on the same theme:

> *Jerusalem, Jerusalem, the city that kills the prophets and stones those who are sent to it!* (Luke 13:34)

An absolute regime will not tolerate voices of dissent.

Already in the Northern Kingdom of Israel, the kings of the Omri dynasty were much vexed by the prophetic soundings of Elijah and Elisha (see 1 Kings 18:4)! Thus, King Ahab identifies Elijah as a "troubler of Israel," one who unnecessarily and unacceptably caused unrest in the realm by his alternative performance (18:17). After the narrative of Naboth's vineyard, moreover, the rhetoric escalates so that the king sees Elijah as "my enemy" (1 Kings 21:20). In the next dynasty in the North, it is a priest in the service of King Jeroboam II who forcefully evicts Amos, the prophet, from the realm, because his harsh word is unwelcome there:

> *O seer, go, flee away to the land of Judah, and earn your bread there, and prophesy there; but never again prophesy at Bethel, for it is the king's sanctuary, and it is a temple of the kingdom.* (Amos 7:12-13)

The dismissal of unwelcome prophetic voices in the North is evident, as well, in the popular verdict concerning Hosea the prophet:

> *The prophet is a fool. The man of the spirit is mad* ["meshugga"]. (Hosea 9:7)

It is "madness" for the prophets to speak a word outside the establishment's approved ideology! Such voices are to be forcefully refused and silenced!

But the absolutism of the Jerusalem regime is even more aggressive than it was in the Northern Kingdom of Israel. The confrontation of the regime and prophetic dissent came to its fullest, most vigorous expression in the final days of the dynasty concerning the presence of Jeremiah in the city. From the outset, Jeremiah had been mandated to speak a critique against the entire Jerusalem establishment and its legitimacy:

> *And I, for my part have made you today a fortified city, an iron*
> *pillar, and a bronze wall,*

> *against the whole land—*
> *against the kings of Judah,*
> *against its princes,*
> *against its priests, and*
> *against the people of the land.* (Jeremiah 1:18)

The repeated preposition "against" makes the point unmistakably. And indeed, this insistent calling to be a critical voice of opposition evoked Jeremiah's practice of complaint in which he protests against the vocation given to him by God (see Kathleen O'Connor, *The Confessions of Jeremiah: Their Interpretation and Role in Chapters 1–25*). He does not want to be mocked and endangered as a constant voice of critique, but he has no escape from his calling:

> *For whenever I speak, I must cry out,*
> *I must shout, "Violence and destruction!"*
> *For the word of the Lord has become for me a reproach and*
> *derision all day long;*
> *If I say, "I will not mention him,*
> *or speak any more in his name,"*
> *then within me, there is something like a burning fire shut up*
> *in my bones;*
> *I am weary of holding it in, and I cannot.* (Jeremiah 20:8–9)

He cannot speak; he cannot keep silent! As a result, his life amounts to a vexed running commentary against the Jerusalem establishment. Early in his public life, he is put on trial for his words. The charge against him is sedition:

> *The priests, prophets, and all the people laid hold of him, saying. "You shall die! Why have you prophesied in the name of the Lord, saying, 'This house shall be like Shiloh, and this city shall be desolate, without inhabitants'?". . . This man deserves*

> *the death sentence because he has prophesied against this city, as you have heard with your ears.* (Jeremiah 26:8–11)

His accusers, most especially the religious leaders, find his words unbearable. In his prophetic imagination, he has dared to anticipate that the royal city would sooner or later be reduced to rubble, as was the old sanctuary site of Shiloh in the North (see Jeremiah 7:12–15). It was intolerable for his contemporaries to dare to imagine such an ignominious ending for the glorious seat of the king and the temple. In the end, Jeremiah is acquitted of the charge of treason by an appeal to an older prophetic parallel (26:17–19; see also Micah 3:12). In the end, he is saved by the decisive intervention of the family of Shaphan, a major political player who had shared with Jeremiah his estimate of the security risks of the city (see 26:24). The priests who accused Jeremiah termed his prophetic judgment "treason" because he voiced reality outside the ideology of the regime.

Later in his prophetic utterance, as the threat of Babylon becomes more specific and ominous, Jeremiah is again taken to task for his report. This time Jeremiah's words used the classic triad of covenant curse to articulate the threat facing the city and the royal-temple establishment:

> *Those who stay in the city shall die by the* sword, *famine, and* pestilence*; but those who go out to the Chaldeans shall live; they shall have their lives as a prize of war, and live.* (Jeremiah 38:2)

The only "positive" alternative the prophet can foresee is a willing surrender to and deportation by Babylon. Again, officialdom, in thrall to the ideology of the king and temple, finds such a threat unthinkable. Furthermore, they propose a death sentence for Jeremiah:

> *This man ought to be put to death, because he is discouraging the soldiers who are left in this city, and all the people, by*

> *speaking such words to them. For this man is not seeking the welfare of this people, but their harm.* (Jeremiah 38:4)

The phrase "discouraging the soldiers" is a translation of the actual phrase, "weakening the hands of the soldiers," that is, undermining the war effort by shaking the troops' confidence. Popular opinion judges that the prophet is not seeking the *shalom* of the city because, for them, the *shalom* of the city is all tied to the ideology of Jeru*salem* through the king and temple.

King Zedekiah refuses the blood-thirsty crowd (38:5). Zedekiah may be a coward. Or he may recognize the limit of royal authority or even sympathize with Jeremiah's counsel. We are not told. Either way, the king declines to exercise royal authority:

> *Here he is; he is in your hands; the king is powerless against you.* (38:5)

The words receive an eerie reiteration on the lips of Pilate, the Roman governor in the case of Jesus (John 19:14–16). Like Zedekiah, Pilate refuses to execute a critic of the dominant ideology. But like Zedekiah, Pilate willingly hands over the one accused to the eagerness of the crowd. Jesus, like Jeremiah, is portrayed as an enemy of the state, as an enemy of Caesar:

> *Everyone who claims to be a king sets himself against the emperor.* (John 19:12)

Paul Lehmann, in *The Transfiguration of Politics: The Presence and Power of Jesus of Nazareth in and over Human Affairs*, writes of this confrontation:

> *The confrontation of Jesus and Pilate underscores the great gulf between* political realism *and* Realpolitik. Realpolitik *is*

> *politics with the accent upon the primary of power over truth.* Political realism *is politics with the accent on the primacy of truth over power.* Realpolitik *increasingly succumbs to the temptation of confusing immediate goals and gains with ultimate outcomes and options and seeks validation by increasingly dubious authority.* (56)

That dubious anxious authority is exhibited in the readiness to label as "treason" every hint of dissent.

I learned from this how readily the dominant regime, based on the dominant ideology, can dismiss dissenters and critics with the label of "treason." I was alert to this recurring theme as I read the critical book by Larry Diamond, *Ill Winds: Saving Democracy from Russian Rage, Chinese Ambition, and American Complacency* (2019). The book's subtitle portrays Diamond's triangular mapping of world power as a hard-ball struggle among Russia, China, and the United States. Diamond's thesis is that authoritarianism is everywhere on the move against democratic governments and that the United States must, with great intentionality, lead democratic nations in the defense and promotion of democracy, or authoritarianism will prevail.

In the second chapter, Diamond writes of the "authoritarian temptation" that leads to an extended exposition of the "authoritarian temptation" of Donald Trump. In his analysis, Diamond outlines the "autocrats' twelve-step program" of a generic kind for the seizure of public power (pp. 64–65). He observes that this is the playbook for contemporary authoritarians, including Hugo Chavez and Recep Tayyip Erdogan. A few pages later, he asserts:

> *Trump's presidency has brought more direct and chilling assaults on the norms and institutions of democracy.* (82)

He offers a list of twenty quite specific actions by Trump, including various assaults on the norms and institutions of democracy (83–84).

He also allows, of course, that many more might be catalogued as well. What caught my eye in this list is Diamond's final item of assaults on democracy:

> *[He] repeatedly brands his foes as traitors—from saying that the* New York Times *had "virtually" committed "treason" by running a critical essay in December 2018 by an anonymous senior administration aide to calling some congressional Democrats "un-American" and "treasonous" for not applauding a passage in his 2018 State of the Union Address.* (84)

The verdict of "traitor" and "treason" can be readily on the lips of Trump as a dismissive label for those who oppose him. Remarkably, the label is available for something as trite as a newspaper essay or, even more ludicrous, for not applauding his speech. Like every authoritarian response, Trump, in his authoritarian response, can readily label any dissent as treason. In his preemptive aggression, Trump stands in the succession of the biblical propensity to label dissent as treason. Trump is aligned with the following:

- King Ahab identified Elijah as a "troubler" and "enemy" (1 Kings 18:17, 21:20)
- the populace that labeled Hosea as a fool and a madman (Hosea 9:7)
- the officials who readily termed Jeremiah a traitor (Jeremiah 26:112, 38:4)
- the crowd that declared Jesus to be "no friend of Caesar" (John 19:12)

"Treason" is an easy dismissal of any voice to the contrary.

And now, as authoritarianism advances in our society, we are legally responsible for speaking out against such authoritarianism by being truth-tellers. Such a responsibility belongs to good citizenship;

it belongs peculiarly to the church because it is, categorically and characteristically, the ultimate rule of God that reduces every would-be absolutism to penultimate status. Thus, I imagine we are variously cast in the role of prophetic truth-telling that we approach with varying degrees of courage or timidity. It cannot be a time for foolish risk-taking. But it also cannot be a time for silence. And as we seek to be truth-tellers, the verdict of "traitor, treason" will be sounded, not only on high but locally and close at hand.

I submit that it is part of the good work of truth-telling to help folk sort out the crucial distinctions among *chauvinism*, *nationalism*, and *patriotism*. I was astonished, as you may have been, to see Roger Stone (the ever-present muse for Trump) say, "I am without apology a Western chauvinist." The Internet easily defines chauvinism in this way:

> *The unreasonable belief in the superiority or dominance of one's own group or people, who are seen as strong and virtuous, while others are considered weak or unworthy, or inferior. . . . a form of extreme patriotism or nationalism, a fervent faith in national excellence and glory.* (https://en.wikipedia.org/wiki/Chauvinism)

Stone's qualifier, "Western," means that his claim is not primarily national (American!); it is, instead, white! This claim among us takes the form of white supremacy and a readiness to engage in violence for that claim. Of course, an exposé of chauvinism will take us some distance toward responses of "treason," just as the biblical witness has it.

Our counter-theme is *patriotism,* a due sense of loyalty to and regard for our national identity as a democracy exercised with critical awareness. We may regard *nationalism* as a halfway house between patriotism and chauvinism, but it is a stance loaded with anti-democratic potential. Most of us are not poised to take on these issues directly. We must not, however, miss our opportunity to bear witness in the face of growing authoritarianism and seductive absolutism. It is exactly the rule of God that presides over all our political posturing. This rule of justice and righteousness, faithfulness and trustworthiness, and compassion is the truth of our life in the public domain. Our witness is to the coming reign of this God that is on the way. It is on the way in such compelling form that even ancient Nebuchadnezzar, amid his absolutism, in his recovering sanity could declare:

> *I blessed the Most High,*
> *and praised and honored the one who lives forever.*
> *For his sovereignty is an everlasting sovereignty.*
> *And his kingdom endures from generation to generation.*
> *All the inhabitants of the earth are accounted as nothing*
> *and he does what he wills with the host of heaven*
> *and the inhabitants of the earth.*
> *There is no one who can stay his hand*
> *or say to him, "What are you doing?"* (Daniel 4:34–35)

This knowing doxology by the king of Babylon anticipates the "loud voices" who dared, amid the empire of Rome, to sing:

> *The kingdom of the world has become the kingdom of our Lord*
> *and of his Messiah,*
> *and he will reign forever and ever.* (Revelation 11:15)

It is with conviction (and often with some misgiving) that we stand in this tradition that refuses every earthly absolute. Such a refusal, in times of emergency such as ours, readily evokes charges of treason. Such are the risks of reperforming in this long-running truth-telling tradition that refuses every embrace of ignorant self-promoting labeling. Truth-tellers refuse to receive the labeling that arises for needy ignorance. All that is required is to remember what has been entrusted to us.

3

WIR SIND DA!

IT IS THE propensity of empires, characteristically, to erase minority populations that they find troublesome, disruptive, or inconvenient. Empires work at such erasure to impose a conformist offer of control over their sweep of power. Empires are impatient with minority populations that do not readily conform to that order. In broad strokes, empires practice two strategies through which they seek to accomplish erasure. On the one hand, they can practice *genocide*, as with US policy toward Indigenous people of North America. On the other hand, they can insist upon *assimilation* whereby minority peoples are required to forfeit their own language, culture, and identity, as with the "church schools" in the United States and Canada that forced Indigenous children into the dominant language and culture. Both strategies of genocide and assimilation have catastrophic impacts on minority populations and their cultural identities.

In light of this framing of the reality of erasure, I will comment on the most remarkable book by Andrew Denson, *Monuments to Absence, Cherokee Removal, and the Contest over Southern Memory* (2017). It is a matter of historical record that the US government, led by Andrew Jackson and reinforced by the state government of Georgia, required the forcible removal of Cherokee tribes in the 1820s via the Trail of Tears. (This is also the decade when the "Doctrine of Discovery" of the Catholic Church was read into US law, giving white Europeans the sole right to territory in the New World.) The forcible removal of the Cherokee tribes resulted in the painful transport west of the Cherokee peoples, away from their native territory.

Beyond that, however, Andrew Denson has traced a most remarkable response to that historic removal on the part of the dominant culture. Rather than the Cherokee peoples being totally "disappeared" to the West (erased), Denson reports on the incredible explosion of monuments to the Cherokee that were erected and established over the territory from which they were removed. Specifically, in New Echota, Georgia, a "model village" of the Cherokee has been erected on a tribal site. That fantastic "model" has been variously replicated through the South, all the way west as far as Arkansas.

Denson reads this remarkable array of monuments to displaced people in an ironic way. It is a way of celebrating those who were here but are no longer here. They are, by the monuments, being remembered so that their land could be cleansed for white settlement. Thus, the several monuments effectively assert white supremacy and white entitlement to the land that no longer belongs to the Cherokee. These monuments to the "disappeared tribes" has the effective irony of being a remembrance of native peoples. At the same time, state legislatures were engaged, as compellingly as possible, in erasing Black populations. The *erasure* of Black folks and the *remembrance* of disappeared Cherokees tilt toward white entitlement, privilege, and supremacy. This historic accomplishment of erasure and memory is breathtaking in its shameless aggression.

Thus, the double irony of *remembrance in the absence* and *Indian memory and Black erasure*! There is, however, a third irony that Denson offers near the end of his book.

> *In 2012, small white signs began appearing next to monuments and roadside markers related to Cherokee history in western North Carolina and southeastern Tennessee. In red letters, printed in both the Cherokee syllabary and English, they stated, "we are still here . . ." The new sign, however, deftly reworked the old, reminding passersby that this place is still Cherokee ground and that the Cherokee people remain present.* (Monuments to Absence, 221)

In the face of white usurpation of land through "disappearance," this ad hoc, unofficial assertion insists that the disappearance and erasure have not been complete or adequate. The Cherokee people, however, reduced in size and power, are still there! The erasure work of empire has a most difficult time completing the task!

> *The signs are offered by a Cherokee artist, Jeff Moody, who intends that the signs would challenge what he termed the "finality" expressed by memorials to Native history created by the dominant society. Historic sites, he observed, suggest that the history of Native peoples has ended.* (221)

Moody's term "finality" inescapably brings to mind the violence of the Nazis who sought a "final solution" to the "Jewish problem." But as the Nazis discovered, and now Moody affirms, such "finality" does not work:

> *History and culture are not static, but grow and develop daily.* (221)

Thus, historical, cultural reality defies administrative closure! Denson concludes that the ad hoc signs

> *politely correct long-established narratives of Indian disappearance. ("By the way," they seemed to remark, "Cherokees did not vanish—this history is not finished.")* (222)

While the land has been taken over and occupied through white violence,

> *Cherokees, however, did not forget. Keepers of traditional knowledge in both the mountains and the West remembered Kituwah and its significance. Tom Belt, who grew up in*

> *Oklahoma and who helped lead the effort to acquire the site, recalls learning of Kituwah from his father and grandmother, who never saw the place. In the mid-1990s, the white family that farmed the land for generations offered to sell the property to the Eastern Band, and, with that act, the mother town returned. After some initial discussion of possible commercial uses for the land, the tribal government decided simply to preserve the site. A few years ago, the Tribal Council passed a resolution affirming Kituwah's standing a sacred place, promising that no new development would occur there.* (226)

This stubborn, insistent assertion of the Cherokee population affirms that white power does not and cannot give closure to Cherokee existence. The Cherokee affirmation, "we are still here," is a refusal of the imperial power of erasure. Denson ends his book with a statement from Principle Chief Joyce Dugan concerning the sacred Cherokee side of Kituwah in North Carolina:

> *The Cherokees who went west on the Trail of Tears, she wrote, "entrusted the preservation of these resources to us." North Carolina Cherokees had the honor and the duty "to protect our homeland until the time they might return. That time is now." Removal was not the end, and Kituwah's people do return. As Belt remarked, "We are only separated by a short distance and a little time."* (227)

This unexpected declaration of the Cherokee people, "We are still here," merits close and sustained attention. This is an affirmation of a minority community that would not be erased. It is an act of defiance against an empire that would erase. And it is a measure of the limit of imperial erasure that the empire itself had thought to be without limitation.

As I pondered this bold Cherokee declaration, I recalled that I had read somewhere (in a reference now lost to me) of a Jewish community under severe assault by the terrorism of the Nazis. In that community, it was the custom of a minion of ten Jewish men to meet in secret as a synagogue practice. Making noise in their meeting was exceedingly risky, so the men sat silently. The silence was only broken, so it was reported, when one of the men whispered, "Wir sind da." The phrase is Yiddish for "We are here." This statement by endangered Jews was a claim closely parallel to that of the last Cherokee assertion.

Similarly, this is the affirmation of another community that it would not be erased. It was an act of quiet defiance against an empire that would erase. And it was a measure of the limit of imperial erasure that the empire itself (in this case, the Nazis) had thought to be without limit in its drive for a "final solution." This whispered utterance declares that there is not and cannot be anything "final" about imperial erasure.

Of course, the Jews, long before the time of the Nazis, were the primary embodiment of a minority community that was troublesome, disruptive, and inconvenient for the empire because faithful Jews refused to meet the expectations of the empire. Thus, long before the ghettos of World War II, Jews have been the perennial subject of erasure. If we push back far enough, we may come to the anticipated erasure of Jews in the Book of Jeremiah in the sixth century BCE. In prophetic parlance, however, Nebuchadnezzar, in the sixth century, is not more than an agent of YHWH who undertakes the erasure (judgment) of the chosen people, Israel. Jeremiah has YHWH speak in a fit of imperial anger that bespeaks the obliteration of all creation and the obligation of Israel as chosen people and Jerusalem as a chosen city. The imperial utterance of YHWH proceeds step-by-step to the dismantling of all of creation, so artistically rendered that it is easy enough to see that the poetic lines are a reversal of the processes of creation in Genesis 1:

I looked on the earth, and lo, it was waste and void;
and to the heavens, and they had no light.
I looked at the mountains, and lo, they were quaking,

and all the hills moved to and fro.
I looked, and lo, there was no one at all,
and all the birds of the air had fled.
I looked, and lo, the fruitful land was a desert,
and all its cities were laid in ruins
before the Lord, before his fierce anger. (Jeremiah 4:23–26).

It is all "before his fierce anger." The lines suggest that the divine erasure is final and complete.

Except that verses 23 to 26, so symmetrically voiced, are followed by verse 27:

For thus says the Lord: The whole land shall be a desolation;
yet I will not make a full end.

Some critics readily read this as a later scribal addition. Perhaps so. Where is it written that the creator God cannot speak as well in a scribal addition? The verse sounds like an afterthought wherein the imperial God reflects on what has just been uttered and finds that, in its harsh finality, it is an overstatement well beyond what the creator God will do, can do, or wants to do. This verse amounts to a retraction by God for what God, in imperial anger, has just resolved. The qualification of verse 27 means that there will not be a "full end" to the chosen people or no complete erasure. We do not know if God cannot do it or will not do it. Either way, God does not do it. It is as though the creator God can hear the chosen people insisting, "Wir sind da." It is as though God attends to the insistent survival of this endangered minority population—Jewish, Cherokee, or whomever.

The historical reality that corresponds to this poetic retraction is found in the last paragraph in Jeremiah (52:31–34; see also 2 Kings 25:27–30). From that narrative report, we learn that even though displaced, disgraced, and rendered helpless, the Jews are still there.

They are still there through King Jehoiachin, who is still in exile, recognized as king:

> *In the thirty-seventh year of the exile of King Jehoiachin of Judah, in the twelfth month, on the twenty-fifth day of the month, King Evilmerodach of Babylon, in the year he began to reign, showed favor to King Jehoiachin of Judah and brought him out of prison.* (v. 31)

Jehoiachin contains the hope and possibility of restoration to the better days that Jeremiah anticipates in his royal body. The Judean king, at the table of the Babylonian king, is an uncompromising assertion, "Wir sind da."

In a very different idiom, the prophet Ezekiel scores the same point against any final erasure of Israel. In three long recitals of Ezekiel, 16, 20, and 23, the prophet imagines the undoing of shameless Israel. These recitals, however, are not permitted as the final word. In Ezekiel 16, after the lengthy rant, 16:59–63 voices a reversal. The God who rants against fickle Israel now speaks in a different mode of covenantal embrace:

> *Yet I will remember my covenant with you in the days of your youth, and I will establish with you an everlasting covenant. . . I will establish my covenant with you, and you shall know that I am the Lord.* (vv. 60, 62)

The point is reiterated in Ezekiel 20. After the long speech of judgment, this same God makes a promise of restoration:

> *For on my holy mountain, the mountain height of Israel, says the Lord God, there all the house of Israel, all of them, shall serve me in the land; there I will accept them, and there I will require your contributions and the choices of your gifts,*

> *with all your sacred things. . . You shall know that I am the Lord, when I bring you into the land of Israel, the country that I swore to give to your ancestors. . . You shall know that I am the Lord, when I deal with you for my name's sake, not according to your evil ways, corrupt deeds, O house of Israel, says the Lord God.* (20:40, 42, 44)

There is, even in these verses, a note of continuing severity. That severity, however, is overruled by a resolve for restoration.

The utterance of these lines of restoration in Ezekiel 16:59–63 and 20:33–44 is not easy to adjudicate. Are they simply "feel good" additions to soften the rhetoric? Or are they, as I think, to be taken as revelatory disclosures of the God who finally will not and cannot erase? Unlike Jeremiah, the ground of hope in Ezekiel is not divine compassion but rather divine holiness wherein God will rehabilitate Israel for the sake of God's reputation. In the end, even Ezekiel, with his harsh rhetoric, cannot arrive at erasure. He cannot because of historical reality; thus, the book of Ezekiel bases its timeline on the chronology of King Jehoiachin, the same king who appears as a sign of royal continuation in the book of Jeremiah. But YHWH in Ezekiel cannot arrive at erasure because the imperial creator of heaven and earth is not given to erasure. Thus, it is a truth inscribed in the very heart of God that history does not end in a "final solution," not for the Jews or the Cherokee. It ends in the hope and prospect of return and restoration. It was so for sixth-century Jews. And it is so for twenty-first-century Cherokees. And for every such vulnerable minority population that lives courageously and in resistance. The God of fidelity is attentive to the affirmation, "Wir sind da," when uttered outside the barbarism of empire. In response to such "Wir sind da," God is attentively engaged!

This remarkable reality that defies Realpolitik's calculations is a matter of immense import for the church. This foil to imperial erasure is an insistence that the "arc of history" is not determined by the force of empire. It is determined by the resolve of fidelity that acts in solidarity with the vulnerable who are repeatedly the targets of erasure. This resolve of fidelity is promised and hoped, can and will and does run beyond the force of imperial erasure.

From all of this, the church is summoned to its work of resistance and witnessing against imperial erasure. It turns out that imperial erasure is a gesture of idolatry because it imagines that the dominant culture, tempted to erasure, can be ultimate in the imposition of its violent will. Because it trusts in the God of the gospel, the church resists any such idolatrous claim of ultimacy. It is the work of the church to embrace those minority populations that are subject to erasure, to provide protection, to valorize their presence in history as active agents of their future, and to remember and cherish the names of those who have been subject to such erasure. Now, in our current season of fascist reaction, there are many populations threatened by erasure. Thus, voter repression is an act of erasure, and gerrymandering election districts is an act of erasure. Violence committed in gay bars is an act of erasure. Laws that deny women control of their own bodies is an act of erasure. The church must stand with and for those populations in both resistance and affirmation.

In Christian confession, the ultimate moment of imperial erasure is on Good Friday. By sundown on that Friday, the emperor, the governor, and the Jewish king, Herod, all thought they had effectively erased and eliminated the threat of the alternative governance that Jesus embodied. We confess, to the contrary, that the one they tried to execute and erase has been restored to life and governance. Thus, the Easter declaration of the Risen Christ is

> *Ich bin da!*
> *I am here!*

We Christians confess that his re-emergence in power validates the claim that God's creation is on its way to newness. The ground for such confidence in God's future is in our confession:

Er ist da!
He is here!

Or as we translate,

Christ is risen!

The erasure by empire has reached its limit on that Friday. This is the ground for refusal and resistance to such erasure, affirming the Cherokee insistence,

> *We are still here . . . History is not finished.* (*Monuments to Absence*, 221–222)

4

WATCH WHERE YOU GO AND HOW YOU GET THERE

In the path of righteousness there is life,
In walking its path there is no death. (Proverbs 12:28)

IF YOU DO not know the work of Norman Wirzba (Duke University), hurry to learn about him and get his books. Wirzba writes the freshest material concerning "the environment"; only he takes it as God's *good, life-giving creation.* He follows in the train of Wendell Berry but writes with a more frontal theological accent. Among his more compelling phrasings is his translation of *creatio ex nihilo* (creation out of nothing) into "creation out of love" (*creatio ex amour*). That alteration changes everything we may think and do about creation care. In his current book, *Agrarian Spirit: Cultivating Faith, Community, and the Land* (2022), Wirzba writes the remarkable words:

> *The first thing to say about a path of genuine transformation is that it is a* path *and not a* road. *Roads are constructions that aim to get people across a place as quickly and efficiently as possible. They tend, as much as possible, to be straight and smooth, which means that the land has to be bulldozed and graded for the road to fit within a predetermined line. Whatever obstacles are in the way must be removed because one's focus is primarily the destination rather than the places along the way. A path, by contrast, is born of a much slower movement and proceeds by direct contact and familiarity with the contours of the land. It meanders, often forks, and prefers to go around obstacles. A path, in other words,*

> *communicates respect, even affection, for a place by showing the willingness of people to adapt their movements to what the place recommends. If, as Berry suggests, a road acts like a bridge that avoids contact with places conceived as abstract spaces, then a path takes people into places that personal experience has taught them to be of value.* (120)

These words are worth a long pondering, in the context of *slowness* and *speed*, and the appreciation of *place* in distinction from abstract *space*.

In the Proverb I have cited above, there is a contrast between *life* and *death*. There are particular distinctions in different directions and speeds of journeying. In much of the Bible, "life and death" are not settled, finished absolutes but are processes of well-being or trouble, prosperity or adversity. The routes and modes of travel are commensurate with outcomes, that is, processes for good or evil. Moreover, the two "points of destination" are linked to the two terms for the travel route. Unfortunately, one cannot tell from the NRSV translation that the words "path" and "path" render different Hebrew terms. The first "path" is *'orah*, the second is *derek*. The first term is consistently used for a "path" that suggests a slow, deliberate, traditional, familiar route of travel. The second, *derek*, is a more common term with a much broader usage denoting a passage from a path to a road, a highway, or a superhighway. While the semantic distinction is not absolute or entirely consistent, it is enough that we can appeal to it to consider the force of the Proverb and reflect on the either/or of wisdom.

This Proverb, like all such Proverbs, reflects on the community's accumulated experience over time. The community has learned, through long trial and error and careful discernment, what kinds of conduct, practice, and policy make for life, prosperity, and well-being for the community. It has learned, at the same time and in the same way, the kinds of behavior, practice, and policy that damage the community. Thus, the many "better sayings" in the wisdom tradition can discern and articulate that some conduct is "better" than other conduct because the "better" conduct produces good outcomes:

> *Wisdom . . . is better than silver,*
> *. . . better than gold.* (Proverbs 3:13–14)

> *My fruit is better than gold, even fine gold,*
> *And my yield than choice silver.* (Proverbs 8:19)

> *Better is a little with the fear of the Lord*
> *than great treasure and trouble with it.* (Proverbs 15:16)

> *Better is a dinner of vegetables where love is,*
> *than a fatted ox and hatred with it.* (Proverbs 15:17)

The wisdom traditions have drawn conclusions over a long period about the better choices to be made, even if those choices seem counterintuitive. Wisdom is to be "on the way" with *better alternatives* that promise *better outcomes* for self and the community. The same decisions are, in a different way with different framing, reflected in the Torah so that the covenant community of Israel is always standing before choices. When Israel chooses "the path" of righteousness, life, and justice, well-being will result. Conversely, the path of *bad choices* produces *bad outcomes* and eventually land loss (see Deuteronomy 30:15–20). Thus, both wisdom teaching and Torah instruction concern the nurture of an aptitude for a life of right choices said to be on "the way of life." Neither wisdom teaching nor Torah instruction suggests that there can be any circumstance in which a "better" choice cannot be made or in which a poorer choice cannot be made with bad outcomes. Thus, the wisdom tradition can speak variously of "the paths of justice" (Proverbs 2:8), "the paths of uprightness" (Proverbs 2:13), "the paths of the just" (Proverbs 2:20), "the path of the righteous" (Proverbs 4:18), and "the path of life" (Proverbs 5:6).

Verses in the book of Jeremiah are a summons to "the ancient paths," the ones tried and tested over time. The prophet does not specify here that path. Still, he sees that the course consists of neighborly practice, especially toward widows, orphans, and immigrants (see Jeremiah 5:28, 7:6). But Jeremiah watched as the royal-priestly leadership in Jerusalem had chosen otherwise. That enterprise chose a vigorously exploitative way of wealth and power. It waged a ruthless economic war against its own peasant community on which it depended for sustenance. Jeremiah summons his community:

> *Stand at the crossroads, and look,*
> *and ask for the ancient paths,*
> *where the good way lies; and walk in it,*
> *and find rest for your souls.* (6:16)

As soon as he issues that summons, however, the prophet promptly attests that his community and its leadership have chosen otherwise:

> *But they said, "We will not walk in it." . . .*
> *"We will not give heed."* (6:16–17)

For the prophet, it follows that such a refusal leads inescapably to the harsh response of a lordly "therefore" of destruction and death:

> Therefore *hear, O nations,*
> *and know, O coastlands . . .*
> *See, a people comes from the land of the north,*
> *a great nation is stirring from the farthest parts of the earth*
> (6:18, 23).

So, consider "paths." They are formed by habit and reiterated walking. Even cows soon trace out a path as they head "home" at milking time after a long day. Such routes take the landscape as it is and traverse it unhurriedly. By contrast, a "road" or, better, "a highway" brings the necessary bulldozers and earthmovers to alter the landscape to make travel swifter and more convenient. This is in the familiar scene offered by the poet as he imagines YHWH's royal return to Jerusalem after the exile:

> *In the wilderness prepare the way* [derek] *of the Lord,*
> *make straight in the desert a highway* [mesillah] *for our God.*
> *Every valley shall be lifted up,*
> *and every mountain and hill be made low;*
> *the uneven ground shall become level, and the rough places a plain.*
> *Then the glory of the Lord shall be revealed,*
> *and all people shall see it together,*
> *for the mouth of the Lord has spoken.* (Isaiah 40:3–5)

Kings do not travel on cow paths! This must be a road that is straight, open, and unimpeded. One gets the imagery of fast horses and chariots or, belatedly, tanks and troops arriving with a show of great power and domination. The same imagery is picked up in the scenario that imagines more specifically, the return home:

> *A highway* [maslul waderek] *shall be there,*
> *and it shall be called a Holy Way* [derek haqodesh];
> *the unclean shall not travel on it,*
> *but it shall be for God's people;*
> *no traveler, not even fools, shall go astray.* (Isaiah 35:8)

This limited-access road is made safe from dangerous wild animals; no one is unclean! But only the Holy Ones belonging to the returning king, even if that company now includes the blind, the deaf, the lame, and the dumb (vv. 5–6). It is a tightly controlled road dominated by the power of the one who returns in splendor and victory.

Beyond that, the tradition can speak of "the king's highway":

> *Now let us pass through your land. We will not pass through field or vineyard, or drink water from any well; we will go along* the King's Highway, [derek hammelek] *not turning aside to the right hand or to the left until we have passed through your territory.* (Numbers 20:17)

> *Let me pass through your land; we will not turn aside into field or vineyard; we will not drink the water of any well; we will go by* the King's Highway [derek hammelek] *until we have passed through your territory.* (Numbers 21:22)

The phrase "King's Highway" refers to the great road that traverses the Fertile Crescent from Egypt to the great kingdoms of the north. Such a "highway" serves two purposes. First, it moved commerce (I noticed recently in crossing the border from Canada back into the States that the passport control of the United States had two lanes open for cars with very long lines and four lanes available for trucks with no waiting time. What counts is commerce!):

> *Tarshish did business with you [Tyre] out of the great abundance of your wares. Javan, Tubal, and Meshech traded with you; they exchanged human beings and vessels of bronze for your merchandise. Bethtogarmah exchanged for your wares horses, war horses, and mules. The Rhodians traded with you; many coastlands were your own special markets; they brought you in payment ivory tusks and ebony. Edom did business with you because of your abundant goods; they exchanged for your wares turquoise, purple, embroidered work, fine linen, coral, and rubies. Judah and the land of Israel traded with you; they exchanged for your merchandise wheat from Minnith, millet, honey, oil, and balm. Damascus*

> *traded with you for your abundant goods—because of your great wealth of every kind—wine of Helbon, and white wool. Vedan and Javan from Uzal entered into trade for your wares; wrought iron, cassia, and sweet cane were bartered for your merchandise. Dedan traded with you in saddlecloths for riding. Arabia and all the princes of Kadar were your favorite dealers in lambs, rams, and goats; in these they did business with you. The merchants of Sheba and Raamah traded with you; they exchanged for your wares the best of all kinds of spices, and all precious stones, and gold. Haran, Canneh, Eden, and merchants of Sheba, Asshur, and Chilmad traded with you. These traded with you in choice garments, in clothes of blue and embroidered work, and in carpets of colored material, bound with cords and made secure; in these they traded with you. The ships of Tarshish traveled for you in your trade.* (Ezekiel 27:12–25; see Revelation 18:11–13)

The construction of great highways was to move the great economy of commodities to satisfy the needs and wants of the wealthy on an international scale. In both Ezekiel 27:13 and Revelation 18:13, the inventory of commodities includes "human beings" (*nephesh adam*) that are enslaved people as part of commercial transactions. The text does not blink at the mention of them. Second, the purpose of the great highways is to move military resources effectively and speedily to maintain political-economic control of land or to expand one's territory where possible. (It may be noted that in Isaiah 19:23–25, the poet can imagine an alternative purpose of the highway through a vision that at the ends of the highway and at every point along the way, the people might live in everyday well-being and faith.)

These roads are marked in two ways. First, they are efficient. They move people and goods through the landscape without having to face any of the impediments of natural or social barriers that might otherwise pose problems. Second, they are designed to move quickly because "time is money." For both *commercial* and *military* purposes, *efficiency* and *speed* count for a great deal. As a result, every well-functioning state, kingdom, or empire can provide an "interstate" that will bypass human communities and remain unhindered by the inconvenient reality of human habitation. As it has turned out in our own case, it is even better if the road system can be designed to destroy "undesirable" neighborhoods of the poor or people of color who are, at best, an inconvenience for the regime of efficiency and speed, and do not in any case usefully participate in the great market of commodity goods. Thus, for example, Robert Caro, in *The Power Broker: Robert Moses and the Fall of New York* (1975), has detailed how Moses, as a city planner in New York, deliberately and carefully built highways through "undesirable" communities in the city to destroy them and to require removal of those populations that served no purpose in his vision for the city. This is undoubtedly not a recent belated phenomenon!

Wirzba calls attention to "paths" that follow the contours of the land in all its variation. Such paths inevitably are marked by two features contradicting a highway's purpose. Such paths are *slow.* I once stayed at a B&B on a rural road in Scotland. It was a one-lane road for two-way traffic, with occasional wide places to stop and let a car go the other way. One had to be on the lookout for one's neighbor, and invariably the passing of the two cars led to a friendly wave. There is no way to hurry on such a path! It follows that such a way of getting there is what we could term *inefficient.* One could not "rush" anywhere, and the one-lane road assured the neighborhood would not specialize in efficiency.

Wendell Berry, in his current book, *The Need to Be Whole: Patriotism and the History of Prejudice* (2022), labels this contrast of "path" and "road" as "industrialism" and agrarianism." In his alert, critical commentary on Robert E. Lee, Berry writes:

> *His significance for my purpose in this book is that he embodied and suffered, as did no other prominent person*

> *of his time, the division between nation and country, nationalism and patriotism, that some of us in rural America are feeling at present. We speak of it now as the difference between industrialism and agrarianism, but it is essentially the same. It is the difference suffered by small farmers, black and white, who have lost their farms because of the national bias in favor of industrial agriculture, which became doctrinal and total after World War II.* (198)

In this wise book, Berry traces out how what he terms "industrialism" has worked aggressively and effectively (efficiently!) to destroy the neighborhood's fabric. Inevitably such *industrial agriculture* comes with *predatory capitalism* that serves and reinforces elaborate investment in *militarism.* It is all of a piece, a package that works mightily against slowness and inefficiency that are indispensable for a viable neighborhood and common well-being. And as Berry sees, the force of "industrialism" is so insistent that it seems inexorable and irresistible. Berry quotes Paul Krugman, who "surrenders" to such industrialism:

> *There are powerful forces behind rural America's relative and in some cases absolute economic decline—and the truth is that nobody knows how to reverse those forces.* (413)

This last sentence is astonishing! It is not true that we do not know how to "reverse" those forces. Of course, we know the way to reverse those forces. What is required is the "path" to *slow, inefficient neighborliness* that allows time for serious face-to-face interaction and takes seriously the well-being of neighbors whose names we might actually come to know.

The contrast between such *paths of neighborliness* and the *roads of speed and efficiency* constitutes a deep and fraught challenge. It is, however, not a new challenge, only one that has escalated in scale and urgency in our time. It is for that reason that I dare to mention that Jesus readily stood in the tradition of a slow path as he summarized his teaching in what we call his "Sermon on the Mount":

> *Enter through the narrow gate; for the gate is wide, and the road is easy that leads to destruction, and there are many who take it. For the gate is narrow and the road is hard that leads to life, and there are few who find it.* (Matthew 7:13–14)

In his exposition of "the way," Jesus surely echoes the words of the introduction to the Psalter that he knew so well:

> *Happy are those who do not follow the advice of the wicked,*
> *or take the path that sinners tread,*
> *or sit in the seat of scoffers;*
> *but their delight is in the law of the Lord . . .*
> *But the way of the wicked will perish.* (Psalm 1:1–2, 6)

Jesus summons his listeners to choose a path that is not much taken. It is a narrow path; that is, its options are exclusionary. It is a hard path with its many demands. We may take the "Sermon on the Mount" of Jesus as a summary and claim for the alternative way. The Sermon on the Mount includes a hope-filled prayer for neighborly forgiveness, an act unlikely in the industrial economy. It includes hard sayings about relationships because it affirms that relationships count for everything. It commends love of enemies. It invites beyond anxiety to the good work of the coming regime of God. It is a way of discipleship that takes "being on the way" as more important than arrival. It is no wonder that "few" take this path. It is no wonder that many take the path to destruction that in our time is marked by endless technological efforts to outflank the quotidian reality of our fragile human bodies and our equally fragile body politic. Jesus knew in his time about industrial militarism. He knew about the Roman Legions that needed good roads for rapid deployment. He understood, moreover, how religious leaders can be easily and readily co-opted for such speedy efficiency.

But he persists, from village to village, from neighbor to neighbor, from need to healing, from food to hunger. It is no wonder that the Roman regime of speed and efficiency would eventually lose patience with him and need to eliminate the threat that he posed to its confiscatory posturing. And so he was executed. But that Friday of execution also turned out to be the terminal point of "the King's Highway." And then, beyond the reach of imperial road builders, the fragile unhurried path of life was reopened on Sunday morning!

What a wondrous, glorious, hard, arduous work for the synagogue and the church to remember the summons of Moses, the wisdom teachers, and Jesus to take "the road not traveled" that teems with life options. You can see folk on this path every day, refusing speediness long enough to notice neighbors, refusing efficiency to make time for a conversation, a gesture, a march, a protest, an investment, or a law . . . all quite time-consuming enterprises . . . our proper use of our time, energy, and resources. This is indeed a "more excellent way" (1 Corinthians 12:31). It is impossible to imagine Jesus or his people being in a hurry! Contrast the priest and the Levite in the narrative who had schedules to keep (Luke 10:31).

In Acts, the early followers of Jesus were eventually called "Christians" (Acts 11:26). Before that, however, long before that, they were *followers of the way*, that is, *the path*:

> *Meanwhile, Saul, still breathing threats and murder against the disciples of the Lord, went to the high priest and asked him for letters to the synagogues at Damascus, so that if he found any who belonged to* the Way, *men or women, he might bring them bound to Jerusalem.* (Acts 9:1–2)

> *When some stubbornly refused to believe and spoke evil of* the Way *before the congregation, he left them, taking the disciples*

> *with him, and argued daily in the lecture hall of Tyrannus.* (Acts 19:9)
>
> *About that time, no disturbance occurred concerning* the Way. (19:23)
>
> *I persecuted* this Way *up to the point of death by binding both men and women and putting them in prison.* (Acts 22:4)
>
> *But this I admit to you, that according to* the Way, *which they call a sect, I worship the God of our ancestors, believing everything laid down according to the law or written in the prophets.* (Acts 24:14)
>
> *But Felix, who was well informed about* the Way, *adjourned the hearing . . .* (Acts 24:22)

The narrative of Acts shows how it was for the "followers of the way." They bewildered the officials because their conduct was so odd, unsettling, and inexplicable. It is still so for this company, *informed by wisdom, propelled by Torah*, and *summoned by Jesus* to take *the path* and avoid "the king's highway" that continues to be an endless seduction for us. The way of that path requires a different set of skills and sensibilities. Here is a catalog of such an alternative skill set:

> *The fruit of the Spirit is love, joy, peace, patience, kindness, generosity, faithfulness, gentleness, and self-control.* (Galatians 5:22–23)

A more excellent way indeed! And more demanding! And riskier! It is a great gift to come down where we ought to be! My teacher, James

Muilenburg, in his elegant way, brings the two accents of "path" and "road" together in his final sentence in *The Way of Israel* (1961):

> *It is the way of Israel to make straight a highway for her God.* (150)

Obedience to Torah is the proper mode of preparation for the arrival of *the emancipatory regime*!

5

TWO FARMERS . . . TWO WAYS

MY FRIEND SHANE Ash and I were leafing through some of our favorite pages in *Jayber Crow, a Novel: The Life Story of Jayber Crow, Barber, of the Fort William Membership, as Written by Himself*, Wendell Berry's most successful book. I opened the book to pages 181 to 185, where Berry contrasts the life and work of *Athey Keith* and that of his son-in-law, *Troy Chatham*. The transaction between the older man and his son-in-law concerned the farm's transmission from generation to generation, a transaction sure to be fraught with tension and ambiguity. Berry takes the trouble to sketch out his characters with some great nuance. Athey, along with his wife, Della,

> *had about them a sort of intimation of abundance, as though, like magicians, they might suddenly fill the room with potatoes, onions, turnips, summer squashes, and ears of corn drawn from their pockets. Their place had about it that quality of bottomless fecundity, its richness both in evidence and in reserve.* (181)

Athey was an old-fashioned farmer whose life was marked by wisdom, frugality, and generosity. He is, of course, Berry's model farmer who cares well for the land:

> *Athey was not exactly, or not only, what is called a "landowner." He was the farm's farmer, but also its creature and belonging. He lived its life, and it lived his; he knew that, of the two lives, his was meant to be the smaller and the shorter.* (182)

Athey easily resisted the temptation to produce "evermore." The yearning for "ever more" by Troy

> *brought Athey to a stop. The law of the farm was in the balance between crops (including hay and pasture) and livestock. The farm would have no more livestock than it could carry without strain. No more land would be plowed for grain crops than could be fertilized with manure from the animals. No more grain would be grown than the animals could eat. Except in case of unexpected surpluses or deficiencies, the farm did not sell or buy livestock feed. "I mean my grain and hay to leave my place* on foot,*" Athey liked to say. This was a conserving principle; it strictly limited both the amount of land that would be plowed and the amount of supplies that would have to be bought. Athey did not save money at the expense of his farm or his family, but he looked upon spending it as a last resort; he spent no more than was necessary, and he hated debt.* (185)

He marveled at the fruitfulness of the land.

> *Athey said, "Wherever I look, I want to see more than I need."* (181)

His son-in-law, Troy, embodied a contradiction of everything Athey understood and valued. Troy always wanted more! He tried to plow more of the farm to have greater productivity. Troy did not mind a little debt, something Athey would never countenance. Troy wanted to plow more of the farm acreage for the sake of greater profit. He did not hesitate to buy a tractor to farm and produce more. He did not mind that the tractor put him in debt. He readily embraced more plowed acreage, debt, expansion, and productivity.

Berry sketches out the contrast between two notions and two practices of farming, the father-in-law and the son-in-law engaged on the same farm acreage:

> *And so the farm came under the influence of a new pattern, and this was the pattern of a fundamental disagreement such as it had never seen before. It was a disagreement about time and money and the use of the world. The tractor seemed to have emanated directly from Troy's own mind, his need to go headlong, day or night, and perform heroic feats. But Athey and his tenant and his tenant's boys were still doing their work with teams of mules . . . The work of the farm went on at two different rates of speed and power and endurance. It became hard to cooperate, not because cooperation was impossible but because the tractor and the teams embodied two different kinds of will, almost two different intentions . . . Little by little, he [Athey] began giving way to Troy's wants and ideas, and the old pattern of the farm began to give way.* (186)

"The tractor and the teams!" What a clear and inerrant expression of contrast, contradiction, and conflict!

Shane and I saw clearly that this sketch by Berry articulates the tension of "two ways" that characterize our life in the world. We are always standing before the "two ways" and needing to decide. It is not a once for all decision, but a daily decision that concerns small things, the sum of which matters cosmically.

This clear distinction between "two ways" that Berry sees clearly is as old as Moses in ancient Israel. In the Sinai covenant and the derivative tradition of Deuteronomy, Moses articulates a decisive either/or that ancient Israel cannot evade. At Sinai, the Ten Commandments constitute a summons to love this God and no other and to love neighbor as self (Exodus 20:1–17). The covenantal tradition of

Deuteronomy details the choices to be made concerning the practice of *holiness* congruent with the holy God and the practices of *justice* toward the neighbor that dictates specific economic practices. In this latter tradition, Moses seeks to fend off the "Canaanite" alternative that seduced Israel away from covenant. The term "Canaanite" in this usage is not an ethnic term but refers to socioeconomic practices in which all of life is reduced to a commodity that can be used to exhaustion, accumulated without end, and that readily turns neighbors into greedy, fearful competitors. In his summary statement, Moses can characterize the way of covenant or the Canaanite alternative as a decision of "life or death," of "prosperity or adversity":

> *See, I have set before you today life and prosperity, death and adversity. If you obey the commandments of the Lord your God that I am commanding you today, by loving the Lord your God, walking in his ways, and observing his commandments, decrees, and ordinances, then you shall live and become numerous, and the Lord your God will bless you in the land that you are entering to possess. But if your heart turns away and you do not hear, but are led astray to bow down to other gods and serve them, I declare to you today that you shall perish; you shall not live long in the land that you are crossing the Jordan to enter and possess. I call heaven and earth to witness against you today that I have set before you life and death, blessings and curses. Choose life so that you and your descendants may live, loving the Lord your God, obeying him, and holding fast to him; for that means life to you and length of days, so that you may live in the land that the Lord swore to give to your ancestors, to Abraham, to Isaac, and to Jacob.* (Deuteronomy 30:15–20)

The reason that this declaration is so urgent is that the "Canaanite" alternative appears to offer a life of ease, comfort, and security, when in fact it is a way of the destruction of self, neighbor, community, and eventually creation.

We can see this either/or reiterated in a great number of Old Testament texts, of which I will mention three.

1. When Israel had been well settled in the land of promise, Joshua leads Israel in a momentous, dramatic process of covenant-making. He summons Israel to choose the God of life and to reject the available alternatives:

> *Now therefore revere the Lord, and serve him in sincerity and in faithfulness; put away the gods that your ancestors served beyond the River and in Egypt, and serve the Lord. Now if you are unwilling to serve the Lord, choose this day whom you will serve, whether the gods your ancestors served in the region beyond the River or the gods of the Amorites in whose land you are living; but as for me and my household, we will serve the Lord.* (Joshua 24:14–15)

Israel is fully prepared to choose the God of the Exodus:

> *Far be it from us that we should forsake the Lord to serve other gods; for it is the Lord our God who brought us and our ancestors up from the land of Egypt, out of the house of slavery, and who did those great signs in our sight. He protected us along all the way that we went, and among all the peoples through whom we passed; and the Lord drove out before us all the peoples, the Amorites, who lived in the land. Therefore we will serve the Lord, for he is our God.* (Joshua 24:16–18)

After Joshua's further warning, Israel is firm and insistent in its decision:

> *No, we will serve the Lord! . . . The Lord our God we will serve, and him we will obey.* (Joshua 24:21, 24)

The outcome of this process is to bind Israel to YHWH in obedience, with a determined rejection of alternative loyalties.

2. In the acute contestation in Israel in the ninth century BCE, the prophet Elijah reiterates the role of Moses. In the dramatic contest of Mount Carmel, Elijah summons Israel, yet again, to a sharp either/or:

> *How long will you go limping with two different opinions?*
> *If the Lord is God, follow him; but if Baal, then follow him.*
> (1 Kings 18:21)

Limping on two opinions is an effort to have it both ways, to have *the "religion" of YHWH* and *the socioeconomics of Baal,* the totem of commoditization. Elijah insists that Israel cannot have it both ways. After Elijah performs his great wonder, Israel responds unambiguously:

> *The Lord indeed is God; the Lord indeed is God.*
> (1 Kings 18:39)

The double affirmation emphatically commits Israel to a covenant with YHWH.

But this dramatic affirmation is confirmed in the subsequent narrative that concerns socioeconomic practice. The Elijah tradition knows that a liturgical affirmation is vacuous if it is not matched by communitarian practice. Thus, 1 Kings 21, the narrative of Naboth's vineyard, presents two different views of the land. The royal presumption (not unlike Troy) is that the land is a tradable commodity to be used for productivity and profit. The resistance Naboth offers to the king is rooted in the conviction (also held by Athey) that the land is a precious inheritance to be kept and protected from one generation to the next, and not available for any market transaction:

> *The Lord forbid that I should give you my ancestral inheritance.* (1 Kings 21:3)

The narrative unfolds with a triumphant outcome for the royal perspective:

> *As soon as Jezebel heard that Naboth had been stoned and was dead, Jezebel said to Ahab, "Go, take possession of the vineyard of Naboth the Jezreelite, which he refused to give you for money; for Naboth is not alive, but dead." As soon as Ahab heard that Naboth was dead, Ahab set out to go down to the vineyard of Naboth the Jezreelite, to take possession of it.* (1 Kings 21:15–16).

Except that Elijah, the great advocate for YHWH in 1 Kings 18, now appears in the narrative in vindication of Naboth and of his view of the land. It takes no imagination at all to see that Naboth is an anticipation of Berry's Athey of whom Berry writes:

> *He was the farm's farmer, but also its creature and belonging. He lived its life and it lived his; he knew that, of the two lives, his was meant to be the smaller and the shorter.* (*Jayber Crow,* 182)

Like Athey's after him, Naboth's life was meant to be shorter than the life of the land he inhabited and belonged to.

3. One can find the same either/or repeatedly in the prophetic tradition of Israel. Here I will take the poetic lines of Amos as a case in point. Through chapter 5, the book of Amos issues a series of imperatives that echo the imperative summons of Moses, Joshua, and Elijah:

> *Seek me and live.* (v. 4)

> *Seek the Lord and live.* (v. 6)

> *Seek good and not evil, that you may live.* (v. 14)

> *Hate evil and love good,*
> *and establish justice in the gate.* (v. 15)

The progression of the rhetoric is from "me" to "YHWH" to "good" to "good" to "justice." The terms are all of a piece. YHWH is the source and embodiment of good; the substance of "good" is justice. The practice of YHWH-based justice is life. All that contradicts this neighbor-inclined justice is anti-life and will end in death.

The corpus of the prophet Amos details how justice impinges upon the practice of money in the community and how a passion for profit and the accumulation of commodities is, in the end, a sentence of death. Thus, Amos, like his covenantal predecessors, offers an exposé of an economy devoted to profit at the neighbor's expense.

Finally, in this sequence of summons to choice, we may notice the summons of Jesus amid his Sermon on the Mount:

> *Enter through the narrow gate; for the gate is wide and the road is easy that leads to destruction, and there are many who take it. For the gate is narrow and the road is hard that leads to life, and there are few who find it.* (Matthew 7:13–14)

The summons is only one word: "Enter." The remainder of these lines constitutes an exposition of the "entry." Jesus invites his listeners to a narrow gate and a hard road. That narrow gate and hard road together bespeak neighborly fidelity that can be costly and risky and, at the outset, is at least inconvenient. The alternative that Jesus rejects is a wide gate and an easy road. The choice voiced by Jesus is one of *life* or *destruction*. Taken by itself, this brief statement offers no substance concerning the choice to be made. But the entire covenantal tradition of Israel and the sum of Jesus's teaching elsewhere make clear that Jesus stands in the same covenantal tradition as his forbearers. In that tradition the way of life is loyalty to the God of covenant expressed as neighborly love that shows up in socioeconomic practice. The practice of socioeconomic justice toward the neighbor is a summons away from self-securing accumulation and the anxious greed that propels it.

We can see that Berry's narrative presentation of Athey and Troy constitutes a stunning reiteration of the same covenantal claim made repeatedly in the biblical tradition. Athey embodies life with a deep attachment to and respect for the land and a positive regard for his neighbors and the neighborhood. Troy, by contrast, has no serious concern for the land, the neighbor, or the neighborhood. Everything for Troy is reduced to commodity; he is free (and compelled!) to pursue the accumulation of more and more without regard to the abuse of the land or disregard of the neighbor. In his delicate narrative art, Berry has relentlessly reiterated the ancient and durable either/or of the covenant.

The either/or uttered by Moses and reiterated by Joshua, Elijah, Amos, Jesus, and Berry, among others, pertains to every sphere of our common life. Most particularly, it pertains to matters of public practice and public policy. We might notice and heed its pertinence to the public sphere, given that we live in an economy where the gap between workers and owners-managers grows and grows and grows without restraint. A socio-economy that gives tax preference to the wealthy, that has a parsimonious, unlivable minimum wage, that offers generous tax-funded grants to big land owners and big oil producers, that is grudging in its support of the needy, and that programmatically destroys its own environment is a society that has chosen death and is engaged in relentless self-destruction. The utterance of the either/or suggests that ours is a very late time to re-choose, but not a time that is too late yet.

As we finished our conversation on these pages from Berry, Shane had the thought that the "two ways" are not simply operative socially. The same either/or is operative within each of us. The "better angels" root for us, but in the end we may choose our *better selves* that are on offer as a gift from the goodness of God.

Wendell Berry has sounded this either/or for a very long time concerning land-care, land production, and love of the land. In *Jayber Crow*, Berry's embodiment of good land management is Athey, who is disciplined and restrained in Berry's rendering. He knows exactly what is happening with the new breed of farmers but does not address Troy directly. We could imagine that amid the land crisis, Athey might break his disciplined restraint and raise the issue directly with Troy. If he did, he might ask questions designed to haunt Troy. He might ask:

> *For what will it profit them to gain the whole world and forfeit their life? Indeed, what can they give in return for their life?* (Mark 8:36–37; see Matthew 16:26, Luke 9:25)

Athey would let the questions ring in Troy's ears!

6

ON THE WAY TO OTHERWISE

*Now faith is the assurance of things hoped for,
the conviction of things not seen.* (Hebrews 11:1)

THIS FAMILIAR VERSE introduces the great roster of those who lived *in* and *by faith*. It is an astonishing verse because it recharacterizes faith in a fresh, compelling way. It suggests what faith is not:

> Faith is not a cognitive proposition;
> Faith is not the recital of creed or formula;
> Faith is not an institutional membership.

Rather, faith is an *active, often risky investment in a future* that is not yet in hand. The inventory of the faithful that follows this introductory verse concerns various risks and investments. All of them, however, for all their differences, are "seeking a homeland" (v. 14) and desire "a better country" that is marked by the rule of God and therefore "heavenly" (v. 16). As "strangers and foreigners on the earth" (v. 13), they held the present loosely for the sake of that future toward which they were drawn in practical, concrete ways.

There are always two good reasons not to hope for a future that remains "not seen." One reason not to hope is despair, which concludes present life circumstances are permanent and inescapable and cannot be changed. Such a view of the present makes it impossible to entertain any thought or possibility for an alternative "homeland." The other reason not to hope is that the present circumstance is so comfortable, enjoyable, and reassuring that it is impossible to be any better. It is possible to think that in our society, our refusal or inability to hope is an odd mix of these two stances, *despair and complacency*. In the recital of Hebrews 11, the practitioners of faith refused despair even as they refused complacency. Rejecting despair and complacency, they looked to an alternative future better than any present circumstance.

So let us notice that we live in a society that is largely incapable of such daring hope. We cannot hope because the vexations around us seem intransigent and beyond challenge. Or conversely, we are incapable of hope because we are reasonably well off, and there is no use in rocking the boat. Thus, the outcome is a society devoid of energizing, enlivening hope. And then let us notice that Christian congregations are set down in the midst of such a *hope-less* society to be a community of hope, that is, a community engaged in risk-taking investments in an alternative future, alternative to the present defining circumstance of despair and complacency.

The practical question is, "For what do we hope?" Or, more precisely, "What would 'a better country' look like?" In the Old Testament we host a "better country" in the Promised Land. In the New Testament, the image of a "better country" is the "kingdom of God" (or alternatively in the Fourth Gospel, "eternal life."). It is essential and inescapable that any valid sketch of that "better country" remains open-ended and elusive, resisting any specific reductionist blueprint. Thus, in the parables of Jesus, "the kingdom of God" is elusively sketched out in various parables, none of which offer exactitude.

The durable insistent question is, "What is a better country?" What is it like, and how is it to be configured? It is such a demanding prospect that propels faith, hope, and risk in our chapter. And now, in a society sated in despair and complacency, the church is a community summoned to entertain that better country. It is the pastoral task (a) to empower the community to sketch out that better country for our time and place and (b) to help shape the work, risks, and investments that may effectively move us toward that better country. This hope (faith!) consists of a *visionary possibility* and *specific practical steps toward the performance* of that visionary possibility.

The practical question of hope can be variously framed in relation to any number of demanding crisis points in our society. In response to every such crisis point, the church can be deployed in two ways, first with *hands-on, face-to-face neighborly engagement* and second with *informed insistent policy engagement.* Mostly, local congregations prefer the former, but the latter is urgent and requires sustained investment from hopers.

This twofold engagement pertains to every such crisis issue before us:

- It pertains to our *climate crisis.* Attentive engagement at the local level with good environmental practices is important. But of course policy formation for the protection of the environment and preservation of resources is urgent.
- It pertains to our *economic crisis.* Attentive engagement at the local level concerns generous neighborly practices. In my community, this includes provisions of food and housing for the economically left behind. But such local efforts, important as they are, are no real solution to the need. What is required is a new policy that makes public resources available for those in dire need.
- It pertains to our *crisis of civic order.* We must have local efforts at shared community well-being, a *sine qua non* among us. But we also need policies that protect public security from raging violence that often turns out to be aggressively racist.

The likely prospect is that Christian congregations will be relatively small and lean in time to come into our society. This is no cause for despair. In truth, church rolls have often been inflated by many names of those who have no serious intention of active risk-taking investment in God's good future. When the church is lean, it is more likely to be focused, energized, and mobilized for its primal practice of hope.

The recital of Hebrews 11 consists of those who have invested in the future in risky ways and were altogether realistic about such risk-taking. Such hope very often does not come to fruition:

> *All of these died in faith without having received the promises, but from a distance, they saw and greeted them.* (v. 13)

The hopers "did not receive what was promised" (v. 39). Of course, it will be that way with our committed hope concerning the environmental, economic, and civic order. Our best efforts will not arrive at certain or full fruition. However, that recognition in verse 39 does not lead to disengagement of despair. It leads rather to verse 40:

> *God has provided something better so that they would not, apart from us, be made perfect.* (v. 40)

What a phrase, "apart from us!" These committed hopers are not remote from us. They are linked to us, and we are connected to them. We are related to each other in the "assurance of things hoped for." The things "hoped for" among us include *a viable environment, a workable neighborly economy*, and a *functioning amiable civic order*. We are linked to them in "the conviction of things not seen." Not yet seen among us is good environmental policy and practice. Not yet seen among us is good economic policy in which neighborly resources sustain and enhance the lives of all neighbors. Not yet seen among us is a reliable civic order not skewed by selfish or violent intent. These matters are not yet seen, but we have a "conviction" that they are promised and are on the way.

It is for good reason that at the end of chapter 11 and the move to 12:1, the writer looks back at the roster of hopers and imagines all those hopers around us, witnessing to their faith and observing ours:

> *Therefore, since we are surrounded by so great a cloud of witnesses, let us also lay aside every weight and the sin that clings so closely, and let us run with perseverance the race that is set before us, looking to Jesus the pioneer and perfecter of our faith.* (12:1–2)

When we engage as risk-taking hopers, we are sustained by a "cloud of witnesses" who remain present and engaged with us. This is the real, functioning "communion of saints." Thus, the linkage of the generations as a sustained act of hope matters decisively. Based on that reliable company of witnesses, the writer issues a wondrous invitational summons:

> *Therefore lift your drooping hands and strengthen your weak knees, and make straight paths for your feet, so that what is lame may not be put out of joint, but rather be healed.* (12:12–13)

We are on the way! We are on our way, refusing despair, refusing complacency, on our way to what is hoped for but not in hand, on our way to what is not seen but embraced with conviction. Our way of being in the world is definitively unlike either the despair or the complacency our society is prone to. Otherwise is promised, and we are on the way with our hands that need not droop and our knees that need not be weak!

Isaiah 40 begins the great poetic scenario of homecoming from exile. It answers the despair that arose in the exile. Some concluded that they had been God-abandoned:

> *My way is hidden from the Lord,*
> *and my right is disregarded by my God.* (Isaiah 40:27)

Those who draw that conclusion of God-abandonment fall into the lethargy of despair:

> *Even youths will faint and be weary,*
> *and the young will fall exhausted.* (v. 30)

It is, however, genuinely otherwise for those who do not give in to such despair. The poet asserts the reality of the creator God:

> *He does not faint or grow weary,*
> *his understanding is unsearchable.*
> *He gives power to the faint,*
> *and strengthens the powerless.* (v. 28–29)

The chapter ends with this lyric of hope:

> *Those who wait for the Lord shall renew their strength,*
> *they shall mount up with wings like eagles,*
> *they shall run and not be weary,*
> *they shall walk and not faint.* (v. 1)

The verb "wait" in this verse is a bit tricky. The Hebrew term *qwh* means to hope! Those who hope are not faint or weary! They are the ones with the energy to fly, run, and walk. This expectation of vigorous energy is a complement to and anticipation of Hebrews 12:12–13. Those who hope may fly, run, and walk because they have no drooping hands or weak knees. All of that depends, however, on having an identity, a vision, and a company that is quite distinct from the large population that traffics in despair and complacency. It is the good, hard work of the church to maintain a different identity, a different vision, and a different company with whom to fly, run, and walk. These are the hopers. They are the ones who run the race with perseverance (Hebrews 12:1). It is not different in Isaiah 40 from the inventory of Hebrews 11, a company with a transformative, transforming legacy.

7

BIODIVERSITY CONTRA BABEL

AS LONG AS we have assumed that the Bible has an anthropological accent, we have and do read the Bible as though the God of the Bible was solely preoccupied with the human project. Thus, we have traditionally given almost exclusive attention to the human person (and traditionally we said "Man") as the crown of God's creation, made in God's image:

> *What are human beings that you are mindful of them,*
> *mortals that you care for them?* (Psalm 8:4; see Genesis 1:25–27)

This reading of scripture was coherent and could be carried through, for Christians, to the salvific work of Christ in saving humanity from its sin.

All of that has changed under the impetus of environmental studies, the climate crisis, and a new appreciation of the non-human creaturely world. As a result, we can give fresh attention to this alternative accent, rediscovering in scripture what has always been there that we had missed because of our reading lens. We can now see that what we thought pertained singularly to human creatureliness has in purview all creatureliness, human and non-human, all of which is gifted from and turned back in praise and gratitude to the creator. Here is one wee probe to see how this newer attentiveness permits and requires us to read scripture differently. Thus, a consideration of Genesis 11:1–9.

This fourth "sin story" in Genesis (after Adam and Eve, Cain and Abel, and the flood) features the quintessence of human pride and power that seek to impose a singular homogeneity upon human language, thus forcing all peoples to submit to the imposition of a centralized power that wants to silence all local variations of human expression. Apparently, the specificity of the narrative is a reference to the recurring imperial power of Babylon with an allusion to the Babylonian ziggurat as a symbol and articulation of hubristic control and governance. But the specificity of the reference does not detract from the more generic critique of centralizing homogenizing human power. The outcome of the narrative is that such an attempt at the formation of a monolith is foiled by the character of YHWH, who opposes such homogeneity, creates confusion, fails to communicate, and so requires a multiplicity of languages. Short story: The creator God opposes and foils the most hubristic attempt at human unity.

The best study of this text known to me is that of Bernhard Anderson, "The Tower of Babel: Unity and Diversity in God's Creation." His study was published in 1977 and republished in *From Creation to New Creation: Old Testament Perspectives* (1994), pages 165–178. Anderson draws this conclusion concerning the narrative:

> *God's will for creation is diversity rather than homogeneity. We should welcome ethnic pluralism as a divine blessing, just as we rejoice in the rich variety of the nonhuman creation: trees, plants, birds, fish, animals, heavenly bodies. The whole creation bears witness to the extravagant generosity of the Creator.* (177)

Anderson allows that the motivation for the tower building in the narrative may not be rebellion against God:

> *Human beings strive for unity and fear diversity. They want to be settled and are fearful of insecurity. Perhaps they do not*

> *pit themselves against God in Promethean defiance, at least not consciously; but in their freedom they are driven, like the builders of Babel, by a creative desire for material glory and fame, and a corresponding fear of becoming restless, rootless wanderers.* (177–178)

In either pride or fear (or both), the drive for human unity, homogeneity, and power operates against God's will for heterogeneity, diversity, and pluralism:

> *There is something very human, then, in this portrayal of people who, with mixed pride and anxiety, attempted to preserve primeval unity. But their intention to hold on to the simplicity of the primeval past collided with the purpose of God, who acted to disperse them from their chosen center.* (173)

It is important not to miss Anderson's prescient observation, already in 1977, concerning "the nonhuman creation: trees, plants, birds, fish, animals, heavenly bodies."

I had this Genesis narrative (and Anderson's study) in my purview as I tried to read the dense, technical book of Dan Saladino, *Eating to Extinction: The World's Rarest Foods and Why We Need to Save Them* (2021). The book is a study of how our "food habits" have contributed mightily to the loss of biodiversity and the death of many myriads of food species. Saladino traces biodiversity loss concerning wild growths, including hadza honey, murnong, bear root, and memang narang, all plants unknown to me. He then considers cereals, vegetables, meats, seafood, fruit, cheese, alcohol, stimulants, and sweets. At the outset of his book, he indicates the political dimension of our food crisis:

> *Food shows us where real power lies; it can explain conflicts and wars; showcase human creativity and invention; account for the rise and fall of empires; and expose the causes and*

> *consequences of disasters. Food stories are perhaps the most essential stories of all.* (3)

He describes the loss of biodiversity as a threat to life on the planet, so biodiversity becomes a crucial practice for human welfare (183). He concludes:

> *The damage we have caused is reversible, endangered species can be saved and ecosystems can be repaired. The science exists; all that is needed now is the political will.* (223)

When we ask what has produced the loss of biodiversity, it is clear that we have to consider *industrial food policies* coupled with the *indulgence of our consumer inclinations*. This combination has made biodiversity an expensive, inconvenient discipline in which we have no interest and have invested no energy or resources. The outcome of such practice is, in Saladino's phrase, "eating to extinction."

Our current food policy and practice intend to grow more food—*bigger, better,* and *faster*—so that we need not and cannot pause to preserve and protect species that fall outside the regime of bigger, better, faster. Such food policies and practices are propelled by profit and clearly have no interest in the sustainability of the biodiversity of creation. Thus, it takes no great imagination to see that *the hubristic monopoly of food production and consumption* is a replay of the Tower of Babel narrative, saturated by human greed and informed by the technological capacity that aims only at a profit. Further, it takes no great imagination to recognize that our consumer habits have almost no interest in food production but are driven by our taste preferences and hyped-up appetites. Thus, the *homogenization of languages* featured in the Babel narrative has its obvious counterpart in the *homogenization of species* in the interest of greater productivity. As the tower-builders excluded languages other than their own and regarded other languages as expendable and disposable, so contemporary food policy and practice can regard foods other than our immediate preferences as expendable and disposable. Thus, the parallel between *ancient language reduction* and our *current practices of species reduction*. And conversely, the limits on such hubris imposed by the holy God will cause a crisis, sooner or later, concerning such indifference to the realities of creation.

I could readily think of two particular scenarios in scripture that feature extravagant food policy and practice. The first is the more-or-less familiar royal regime of Solomon, who is, in the narrative, celebrated for wealth, power, and extravagance:

> *Solomon's provision for one day was thirty cors of choice flour and sixty cors of meal, ten fat oxen and twenty pasture-fed cattle, one hundred sheep, besides deer, gazelles, roebucks, and fatted fowl.* (1 Kings 4:22–23)

That is a lot of meat! This food practice was made possible, in verse 24, by the "dominion" that Solomon exercised over his known world. Notably, the narrative voices no critique of Solomon's greedy extravagance in food, except that we may recognize that the entire Solomon narrative is likely offered in an ironic tone to suggest what has gone wrong in Israel due to royal hubris and greed. (See Walter Brueggemann, *Solomon: Israel's Ironic Icon of Human Achievement*).

In a second case, we have an exposé of the extravagance of Babylonian [who else?] food practice. In Daniel 5, we are given a scenario of the luxury of imperial food practice:

> *Under the influence of the wine, Belshazzar commanded that they bring in the vessels of gold and silver that his father Nebuchadnezzar had taken out of the temple in Jerusalem so that the king and his lords, his wives, and his concubines might drink from them. So they brought in the vessels of gold and silver that had been taken out of the temple, the house of God in Jerusalem, and the king and his lords, his wives, and*

> *his concubines, drank from them. They drank the wine and praised the gods of gold and silver, bronze, iron, wood, and stone.* (Daniel 5:2–4)

The repeated particular accent on the identification of the vessels as extracted from the Jerusalem temple adds to the insult of the banquet. It underscores the contrast between the *holy practice of the Jerusalem temple* and *the shameless self-indulgent insatiable greed of Babylon* that is undeterred by the holy character of the vessels they utilized.

But that extravagant self-indulgence is inscrutably interrupted by the handwriting on the wall that for a good reason evoked great fear among the royal revelers:

> *Then King Belshazzar became greatly terrified, and his face turned pale, and his lords were perplexed.* (v. 9)

The greedy eaters had assumed that their self-indulgent food practices were secure and could proceed without hindrance. They had, however, failed to reckon with the claims and reality of the holy God who moves against such food policy and practice in hidden but devastating ways. What follows in Daniel's interpretation is the undoing and dismantling of the powerful empire that has had its banquet sharply and enigmatically disrupted.

In a less dramatic but related matter in Daniel 1, the Jewish interns for Babylonian civil service are invited to the "royal rations of food and wine" (1:8). But Daniel and his three Jewish companions refused participation in the imperial indulgence. They are permitted to eat vegetables and drink water instead of the royal menu (v. 12). They prosper because of their disciplined Jewish way that would have no part of the imperial food enterprise. Royal tables are always filled with extravagance. The covenantal-prophetic tradition of Israel characteristically eschews such practice and offers an alternative that is in sync with the realities of our creaturely existence. Now, as then, we may watch as the tower of hubris operates toward *the homogenization of food* and disregards *the holy insistence on biodiversity* that honors every species in our creaturely world.

It is conventional, in Christian interpretation, to twin the narrative of Genesis 11:1–9 with the report of Pentecost in Acts 2:1–13. Whereas Babel attempted a monolith of its dominant language that sought to silence all alternatives, the work of the Spirit at Pentecost is to permit, evoke, and accept the speech of faith in many languages:

> *And at this sound the crowd gathered and was bewildered, because each one heard them speaking in the native language of each. Amazed and astonished, they asked "Are not all these who are speaking Galileans? And how is it that we hear, each of us, in our own native language? Parthians, Medes, Elamites, and residents of Mesopotamia, Judea, and Cappadocia, Pontus and Asia, Phrygia and Pamphylia, Egypt and the parts of Libya belonging to Cyrene, and visitors from Rome, both Jews and proselytes, Cretans and Arabs—in our own languages we hear them speaking about God's deeds of power." All were amazed and perplexed, saying to one another, "What does this mean?"* (Acts 2:6–12)

This capacity for a multi-language community is the work of the Spirit that with the power of the creator overrides all conventional boundaries and makes a new common life possible. *Mutatis mutandis,* we may entertain the thought that it is exactly the work of the Spirit, the work of the creator God, to provide and insist upon biodiversity and the preservation and protection of species. Just as Babel sought to reduce language to a single one that exercised control, so the industrial food project—coupled with undisciplined consumer yearning—aims to minimize species in the interest of speed, quantity, and profit. But the Spirit will have it otherwise because the creator God is insistent upon the teeming myriad of species that refuses our mindless, undisciplined reductionism (see Genesis 1:20–25; Psalms 104:1–23, 27–28, 145:15–16).

Saladino has assured us:

> *The damage we have caused is reversible, endangered species can be saved and ecosystems can be repaired. The science exists; all that is needed now is the political will.* (223)

We may anticipate that it is the Spirit of the creator God who will empower us to refuse and resist our wanton reduction of species. It remains our work to protect and advance biodiversity. But if all that is lacking is the political will, it may indeed be the Spirit that evokes political will for the Spirit has, in every generation, "rushed upon" some of us to move us beyond our conventional assumptions and our conventional preferences to risk for the sake of more generative action. It seems clear enough that *biodiversity* is the creator's will, even as *a multi-language community* turned out to be the will of the Spirit.

8

AN ICONIC ACT OF CIVIL DISOBEDIENCE

> *If you besiege a town for a long time, making war against it in order to take it, you must not destroy its trees by wielding an ax against them. Although you may take food from them, you must not cut them down. Are trees in the field human beings that they should come under siege from you? You may destroy only the trees that you know do not produce food; you may cut them down for use in building siegeworks against the town that makes war with you, until it falls.* (Deuteronomy 20:19–20)

THIS CURIOUS AND remarkable text occurs in Deuteronomy amid a cluster of provisions concerning "holy war." Moses knows that war is a violence waged against an enemy population; he knows as well that it is always war waged against the generative ordering of creation. Already on the third day of creation, we have this:

> *Then God said, "Let the earth put forth vegetation: plants yielding seed, and fruit trees of every kind on earth that bear fruit with the seed in it." And it was so. The earth brought forth vegetation; plants yielding seed of every kind, and trees of every kind bearing fruit with the seed in it. And God saw that it was good.* (Genesis 1:11–12)

God, moreover, charged the first humans with the care of plant vegetation:

> *God said, "See, I have given you every plant yielding seed that is on the face of all the earth, and every tree with seed in its fruit; you shall have them for food . . . I have given every green plant for food."* (Genesis 1:29–30)

The problem is that the makers of war do not pause to consider the creator's will concerning plant life, nor the requirement of protection of plant life that produces food. Our verses in Deuteronomy, it appears, are to be read in the wake of the Genesis provision. The text in Deuteronomy begins with an absolute (apodictic) prohibition against cutting trees. The ban is informed by the recognition that the trees produce fruit that may not be taken. The prohibition is followed by a rhetorical question that insists upon a distinction in a war between human beings and trees. We may hunch that trees are insistently "conscientious objectors" in every war. Human beings are often prone to war, but not trees! Trees are to be given a pass in every war because the creator has provided them for food.

But then in verse 20, the absolute prohibition of verse 19 is qualified with the preposition *raq:* "except." Moses distinguishes between fruit trees that yield food and other trees that do not yield food that may be utilized for the conduct of war. The *absolute prohibition* and the *qualification* that follows together exhibit the characteristic work of Torah teaching that must mediate between absolute theological, covenantal claims and the reality of lived life. What is not "excepted" in verse 20 is the awareness that human life, ultimately and eventually, relies on the food-yielding generosity and fidelity of the creation according to the will and purpose of the creator. The compulsion to make war must be restrained at that non-negotiable limit.

This text has been on my mind because I live in a beautiful tree-laden town that is always threatened by developers who regularly want to cut down more trees and claim more space for more buildings and investment. The tension between tree protection and ongoing development is an enduring contestation in our town. It occurs to me that perhaps the developers in our town are willy-nilly cast in the role of war-makers who wage war against trees and much else in the natural environment without restraint. As one can see, the Torah provision is engaged in delicate negotiation concerning what is allowed and what is prohibited, so in our time the same engagement is underway in our town. I suggest that Moses would have said that the needs of war too often prevail, as one might, in our town, conclude that the war undertaken by the developers too often prevails against the vulnerability of the trees.

We may take a brief glimpse at the parabolic poetry of Ezekiel 17. In that parable, a "great eagle," Nebuchadnezzar of Babylon, takes off the tip of the cedar tree (that is, he deposed King Jehoiachin in Jerusalem) (v. 3). But he cared for this royal remnant in exile so that it flourished (v. 6). But then another "great eagle" (Pharaoh) came and took up the flourishing plant (vv. 7–8). And then, the poet has God ask his Israelite listeners three questions about the judgment made concerning the second great eagle:

> *Will the eagle not tear out the vine by its roots?*
> *Will he not strip off its fruit and cause its leaves to dry up?*
> *Will not all of its fruit and leaves shrivel up?*
> (Daniel Block, The Book of Ezekiel, Chapters 1–24, 1997)

As Block clearly sees, we may imagine those who heard the parable would answer, "Yes," "Yes," "Yes." Yes, the great eagle will work havoc with the tree that is Israel! This usage by Ezekiel is yet another example of how the imagery of the tree lets us see and note clearly how great political, economic, and military power is unrestrained in its exploitation of creation. It does damage to the land itself as well as to its human habitation. We may judge that the siege weapon in Deuteronomy 20:20, unrestrained developers in my town, and the "great eagle" work in the ancient world are all of a piece. All of them regard the momentary gain of wealth and power as so urgent and overriding that they will not pause to consider either the creator's will or the landscape's well-being.

None of the awarenesses of Deuteronomy, my hometown, or Ezekiel's great eagle had prepared me for the moving exposition of "slow violence" of which Rob Nixon (*Slow Violence and the Environmentalism of the Poor*, 2011) writes with such wisdom, courage, and passion. Nixon's general thesis is that the abuse of the environment amounts to slow violence against the most vulnerable human population of the earth. It is "slow" because it advances only by general policies and actions that often remain unnoticed until it is too late; it is "violent" because it abuses the landscape and renders the life of the vulnerable more and more nearly unlivable. Nixon's book, a slow, demanding read, is one to which attention must be paid. In the book, he is not precisely attentive to the vulnerable populations but to the daring, courageous writers who have given voice to the slow violence and the threat against the poor. From my reading of his book, I have acquired a new extensive reading list of books about which I had not known. I urge the reader to pursue the book as a huge wake-up call concerning the jeopardy of land and people we are mostly unaware of. Nixon's book provides chapter and verse concerning the threat in a deeply compelling way.

Among the instances of such slow violence that Nixon considers, I call attention especially to the Green Belt Movement in Kenya, an assertive act of resistance and alternative to the rapacious land treatment by the governing regime. I have not yet read the book that Nixon cites, but I will do so soon. It is entitled *Unbowed*, a memoir by Wangari Maathai, who helped to evoke the Green Belt Movement and has written about her experience with it. The work of the movement was to plant trees. On Earth Day in 1977 Maathai, a "small cohort of like-minded women planted seven trees" (129). By 2004 when Maathai was awarded the Nobel Peace Prize, the movement had created 6,000 local tree nurseries. It engaged 100,000 women to plant thirty million trees in Kenya and elsewhere in Africa. Nixon notes that the achievement of the movement has been *material:*

> *. . . providing employment while helping anchor soil, generate shade and firewood, and replenish watersheds.* (129)

It has also been compellingly *symbolic:*

> *. . . by inspiring other reforestation movements across the globe.* (129)

Nixon labels the movement as "an iconic act of civil disobedience" that has refused to accept "illicit deforestation" perpetrated by Kenya's draconian regime. The movement, not surprisingly, has fostered a broad alliance around issues of sustainable security. These issues, Nixon avers, are crucial,

> *to the very different context of post-9/11 America as well, where militaristic ideologies of security have disproportionately and destructively dominated public policy and debate.* (129)

The outcome of this remarkable enterprise is an

> *alternative narrative of national security, one that would challenge the militaristic, male version embodied and imposed by authoritarian rule.* (128–129)

It cannot be overstated that the movement is led and implemented by women who, in principle and specifics, know what the costs of militarism-cum-deforestation (almost always led by men) are for both land and people.

As a reader, I invite you to ponder the Torah provision requirement, *the development crisis* in my hometown, as in many other places, the threat posed by the *second "great eagle"* in Ezekiel, and the *future of the forests of Kenya.* It is all of a piece. It is all an ongoing relentless contest between the proper caretakers of creation and the convergence of aggressive militarism, predatory economics, and the politics of hubris. The latter converge to regard creation as a tool for their fear, anxiety, greed, and ready violence. The amazing reality in Kenya (that Moses already had in purview) is that resistance and alternative are possible, but such resistance requires sustained courage and daring imagination. Martin Luther has sometimes been attributed for saying, "If I knew that tomorrow the world would go to pieces, I would plant a tree."

I do not know if Luther would regard such an act as "an iconic act of civil disobedience," but it would be nothing less than that. And given Luther's acute sense of drama, he likely would have taken it in exactly that way. Such an iconic act of civil disobedience is surely what James C. Scott (*Weapons of the Weak: Everyday Forms of Resistance*, 1985) means by his title phrase, the capacity of the vulnerable and the resourceless to resist and fight back against great odds in a way that does not lead to punishment or retaliation. It is surely time for the church to educate people about such iconic acts of civil disobedience. A host of insistent women in Kenya compellingly understands the matter. Such a host of brave women is an alternative to those who would destroy our planet in their fearful greed. It has turned out in Kenya that the regime was powerless in the face of tree-planting women. Nixon rightly judges that such issues are crucial in an era of Kenyan authoritarian rule and among us in our "developed" context. Thus, we can see that Moses was well ahead of his time, as he is so characteristically, when he declared:

> *You must not destroy its trees by wielding an ax against them.*
> (Deuteronomy 20:19)

Part II

THE EMANCIPATION OF THE CHURCH

9

SAVED IN AND THROUGH WEAKNESS

I RECENTLY SUBMITTED a prayer for publication in a collection that appealed to "the weakness of God." A copy editor wrote a marginal note for me, observing that "God is not weak." The editor then proposed an alternative phrasing that assigned weakness to those who respond to God, thus transferring "weakness" from God to God's human partners and subjects. And of course, the church has a powerful legacy, including its hymns, of affirming that God is strong:

> *I am weak but Thou art strong;*
> *Jesus, keep me from all wrong;*
> *I'll be satisfied as long*
> *As I walk, let me walk close to Thee.* ("Just a Closer Walk with Thee")

The comment of the copy editor has led me to reflect more upon the notion of God's weakness. There is no doubt that the Bible attests to the power of God (as in the defeat of Pharaoh). That same majestic power, moreover, is evident in the capacity of Jesus to govern even the demons. Such an accent on the power of God has been a long-running seduction for the church, as we have imagined the power of God to be not unlike the worldly influence of mighty empires and imperial rulers. Insofar as the church has been seduced in this regard, attentiveness to the "weakness of God" may be a deep and significant corrective. Thus, my rumination in what follows.

I had in mind three accent points when I considered the "weakness of God."

1. Paul's lyrical summons to the church in 1 Corinthians 1:18–31 is a great exposition of the weakness of God. The "message about the cross" is "to us who are being saved," the power of God. This is the central truth and the core claim of the Christian faith that the crucifixion of Jesus is the performance of God's power that is unlike any capacity in the world. In his exposition, Paul works on a pair of themes:

> The wisdom of the world . . . *the foolishness of God;*
> The strength of the world . . . *the weakness of God.*

To this pair may be added, to complete the triad,

> The wealth of the world . . . *the poverty of God:*

> *For you know the generous act of our Lord Jesus Christ, that though he was rich, yet for our sakes he became poor, so that by his poverty you might become rich.* (2 Corinthians 8:9)

Before he finishes his exposition, Paul, not surprisingly, will go on to trace out the implications of this declaration about God for the life and practice of the church:

> *Consider your own call, brothers and sisters: not many of you were wise by human standards, not many were powerful, not many were of noble birth. But God chose* what is foolish *in the world to shame the wise; God chose* what is weak *in the world to shame the strong; God chose* what is low and despised *in the world, things that are not, to reduce to nothing things that are.* (1 Corinthians 1:26–28)

We may judge, moreover, that this entire riff by Paul is a commentary on the triadic formulation of the prophet Jeremiah:

> *Thus says the Lord:*
> *Do not let the wise boast in their wisdom,*

> *do not let the mighty boast in their might,*
> *do not let the wealthy boast in their wealth;*
> *but let those who boast boast in this, that they understand and know me, that I am the*
> *Lord; I act with steadfast love, justice, and righteousness*
> *in the earth, for in these things I delight, says the Lord.*
> (Jeremiah 9:23–24)

Jeremiah sets up two triads: the world's wisdom, might, and wealth, and the *steadfast love, justice,* and *righteousness* in which the creator God delights. The second triad in Jeremiah does not speak directly of Paul's foolishness, weakness, and poverty. Still, the three relational-covenantal terms move in the same direction of vulnerability, contrasting decisively with the triad of worldly "virtues." Thus, the weakness of God is central to the differentiation of the work and being of God, contrasted to the way of the world of predatory greed. The point is reiterated by Paul at the end of his letter:

> *It is sown in dishonor, it is raised in glory. It is sown in* weakness, *it is raised in power.* (1 Corinthians 15:43)

In this text "weakness" is the way of crucifixion as power is the way of resurrection. The point, moreover, is reiterated in Hebrews 5:2 as well.

> *He is able to deal gently with the ignorant wayward, since he himself is subject to weakness.* (Hebrews 5:2)

2. Thus, the shape of 1 Corinthians is from *crucifixion* in chapter 1 to *resurrection* in chapter 15. The pivot of Paul's reasoning is the centrality of the cross, so that we are led to Good Friday as the great performance of the saving weakness of God. On that Friday Jesus is in the hands of the power of Rome. It will of course be asserted that no one can take

his life from him. In this instant, however, Rome exercised power over his body in a way that left him abandoned.

In his magisterial exposition of Good Friday, Juergen Moltmann, *The Crucified God* (1974), prefers to talk about the "homelessness" and "abandonment" of the Son. And from that he readily concludes that as the Son is homeless, so the Father is also homeless:

> *To understand what happened between Jesus and his God and Father on the cross, it is necessary to talk in trinitarian terms. The Son suffers dying, the Father suffers the death of the Son. The grief of the Father is just as important as the death of the Son. The Fatherlessness of the Son is matched by the Sonlessness of the Father, and if God has constituted himself as the Father of Jesus Christ, then he also suffers the death of his Fatherhood in the death of the Son.* (243)

The emergence of life-giving power in the world can and will arrive only after the deep riskiness of weakness. Moltmann, so far as I know, does not speak of "weakness." But it is surely implied in his daring imagery of *forsakenness.* Jesus is done in by the unflinching power of Rome. In that dramatic moment the weakness of God is no match at all for the power of the empire. Good Friday is the exhibit and the enactment of the weakness of God.

3. This claim for Friday, so central to Paul's evangelical reasoning, has its remarkable substantive counterpoint in the gospel narrative. In his gospel Mark reports on Jesus's presence in his hometown of Nazareth:

> *And he could do no deed of power there, except that he laid his hands on a few sick people and cured them. And he was amazed at their unbelief.* (Mark 6:5–6)

The text is quite explicit: "Could do no deed of power" (*ouk edunato ekei poesesai*) "was not able." It is essential to note that the negative "not able" utilizes the same term in "deeds of power" (*oudemian dunamin*). He had no power to be powerful. The next verse specifies their "unbelief," but it is not parsed as cause-to-effect. His performance in Nazareth simply bespeaks his weakness. The matter is softened in the parallel text of Matthew:

> *And he did not do many deeds of power there, because of their unbelief.* (Matthew 13:58)

The Greek is *ouk epoisesen.* The formulation in Matthew asserts that he did not do acts of power "because of their disbelief." That formulation, however, may mean only that he refused to act in the face of their lack of faith. It does not say that such a lack of faith prevented his action. Nor does it say he "could not." Thus, the matter is left starkly unresolved. We might conclude from these verses that the matter of healing by Jesus is a dialogical act; if the other party is not fully engaged in the act, there can be no restorative outcome. Either way, we are in a moment of the weakness of Jesus. Thus, if we take the trouble to consider the *force of Good Friday*, the *exposition of Paul*, and the *witness of the gospel narrative*, we are led to see that Jesus is portrayed as exercising a kind of power other than unilateral, imperial, or preemptive. His capacity is fully shadowed by the mark of weakness while performed in the world of alternative power.

Here I will pause to reflect on one odd parallelism to the direct contestation of power in the Exodus narrative. In Exodus 7:14–25 and 8:1–15 Moses and the Egyptian "magicians" perform to a draw concerning water-to-blood and frogs. Regarding the third plague of gnats, however, the Egyptian magicians cannot compete with the power of Moses. After Moses and Aaron produce gnats, it is reported:

> *The magicians tried to produce gnats by their secret arts, but they* could not. (Exodus 8:18)

The Greek reading is *ouk edunanto*, "could not"! The phrase is closely parallel to that of Mark concerning Jesus. Of course, everything else is different in the two contests. I cite the Exodus parallel only to call attention to the reality that even strong Pharaoh had limits and came to an insurmountable weakness. Beyond the obvious parallel, everything is different. The Exodus narrative aims to exhibit God's power and the capacity to work for emancipation in the face of hard-hearted Pharaoh. The gospel narrative, by contrast, witnesses Jesus on the way to the cross in his pilgrimage of weakness and vulnerability. But the usage in the gospel narrative has one eye on the old Exodus narration.

The payout of this threefold articulation of the weakness of Jesus is the conclusion to be drawn about the community that seeks to follow Jesus in his weak power. In the Pauline exposition, the articulation of the *foolishness and weakness of God* that counters the wisdom and strength of the world moves from verse 26 toward the church community. It is the church that is to act out the *foolishness and weakness of God:*

> *God chose what is low and despised in the world, things that are not, to reduce to nothing things that are, so that no one might boast in the presence of God. He is the source of your life in Christ Jesus, who became for us wisdom from God, and righteousness and sanctification and redemption, in order that, as it is written [in Jeremiah 9], "Let the one who boasts, boast in the Lord."* (1 Corinthians 1:28–31).

The church consists in those who have no claim to make about wisdom or about might or, for that matter, about wealth. All these worldly insignia are distractions from the single source of "your life in Christ Jesus."

We can see this accent articulated concretely in the church's life. Paul himself can freely acknowledge his own weakness and dependence upon the truth of the gospel:

> *If I must boast, I will boast of the things that show my* weakness. *The God and Father of the Lord Jesus (blessed*

> *be he forever!) knows that I do not lie. In Damascus, the governor under King Aretas guarded the city of Damascus in order to seize me, but I was let down in a basket through a window in the wall, and escaped from his hands.* (2 Corinthians 11:30–33)

Paul adds compelling specificity to his grand gospel claim. It must indeed be weakness to need to be rescued "in a basket through a window in the wall!"

> *On behalf of such a one I will boast, but on my own behalf I will not boast, except of my* weaknesses . . . *He said to me, "My grace is sufficient for you, for power is made perfect in* weakness.*" So, I will boast all the more gladly of my weaknesses, so that the power of Christ may dwell in me. Therefore I am content with* weaknesses *[plural!], insults, hardships, persecutions, and calamities for the sake of Christ; for whenever I am weak, then I am strong.* (2 Corinthians 12:5, 8–10)

For Paul the notion of "weakness" is not a therapeutic ploy, but a real-life experience. The matter is articulated as well in the letter to the Hebrews:

> *For the law appoints as high priests those who are subject to weakness, but the word of the oath, which came later than the law, appoints a Son who has been made perfect forever.* (Hebrews 7:28)

Jesus as high priest follows in the train of those who are "subject to weakness."

This entire exposition bears witness to the reality that God's power for life is not in any way like the power of the world. It is a form of power that proceeds in vulnerability and fragility. And from this it follows that the power of God offered to the church is not like the power of the world. All too often, the church has sought to imitate the power of the world in its wealth, grandeur, pomp, and affluence. Protestantism in the United States has known enough of the worldly exhibit of power in the church. And now that same seduction seems operative in some mega-congregations of so-called "evangelicalism." We can see some of the most egregious examples of this seduction in *Jesus and John Wayne* by Kristen Kobes Du Mez.

These themes of weakness, vulnerability, and fragility are evident among us as we witness and experience the deconstruction of the church as we have known it. In a series of helpful books, Conrad Kanagy (e.g., *A Church Dismantled: A Kingdom Restored*, 2021; *Ministry in a Church Dismantled*, 2021) has traced the dismantling of the institutional church that is all around us in US society. That process will of course be anxiety-producing indeed. But the church of "evangelical weakness" is a compelling reminder to us that our attraction to wealth, power, influence, or grandeur is all a colossal mistake. Thus, the "dismantling" may be an opportunity to flourish in weakness. Such dismantling is not an invitation to withdrawal or retreat into safety and self-defense. It is rather an opportunity to think again about how vulnerability is a great gift in a fearful society. In its vulnerability and weakness, the church has a chance for the work or emancipation and restoration, because it need not be implicated in the violence, intrigue, and greed that so mark the world of predatory power. It is enough to have ringing in our ears the assurance, "My grace is sufficient for you." It is hard work to translate that bottom-line assurance into actual practice. Such a translation summons us out beyond many of our assumptions concerning what it means to be the church in a society that delights in flexing its muscles of power and control.

10

I BET ON YOU

JUSTICE FELIX FRANKFURTER was on the Supreme Court for a long time in a somewhat irascible manner. He was the master at networking and at spotting talent. He identified many gifted students at Harvard Law School and actively and effectively supported their careers. He understood himself to follow in the succession of Justice Oliver Wendell Holmes Jr. and Louis Brandeis, each of whom urged "judicial restraint" and insisted that the court not preempt the law-making responsibility of Congress by being activist on the court. Frankfurter regarded Holmes as the model justice he wanted and tried to emulate. In his welcome biography of Felix Frankfurter, *Democratic Justice: Felix Frankfurter, the Supreme Court, and the Making of the Liberal Establishment* (2022), Brad Synder reports that Justice Frankfurter wrote to William Coleman, his law clerk. It was

> *"a joy to have worked with you for the year, and I shall watch you with great hopes." A year later, he wrote Coleman: "What I can say of you with great confidence is what was Justice Holmes's ultimate praise of a man, 'I bet on him.' I bet on you, whatever choice you may make and whatever the Fates may have in store for you."* (523)

Frankfurter, and Holmes before him, not only bet on such promising young lawyers but mentored and energized them, promoted them, and helped them to supportive professional relationships.

Later on in speaking of Frankfurter's tenacious loyalty to his selected favorite students, Snyder writes:

> *The Red Scare had destroyed Hiss's reputation beyond repair, and, in the process, had damaged Frankfurter's liberal network. Nothing, however, could shake Frankfurter's loyalty to his former students, whether they became secretary of state like Dean Acheson or a convicted felon like Alger Hiss. He was invested in their lives and their careers and considered them surrogate sons. He stood by them during their successes and failures. He bet on them.* (547)

This formula repeated from Holmes has drawn my attention. I have reflected on what it means that an adult with authority and maturity should bet on a younger person. The phrase has interested me as I have pondered my five grandchildren as they find their way to adulthood. I imagine it is the business of grandparents to bet on their grandchildren, and more generally for older people to bet on younger people in effective ways to invite them to find meaningful, significant, well-lived lives.

When I took Holmes's phrase to the Bible, as is my wont, I was led to think about the familiar—and the unfamiliar—story of Samuel. The familiar part of Samuel's story is lovely and idyllic. It begins, as so many biblical birth narratives, in barrenness (1 Samuel 1:2). Hannah yearns for a son and promises that her son would be rigorously obedient to YHWH:

> *O Lord of hosts, if only you will look on the misery of your servant, and remember me, and not forget your servant, but will give to your servant a male child, then I will set him before you as a Nazirite until the day of his death. He shall drink neither wine nor intoxicants, and no razor shall touch his head.* (1 Samuel 1:11)

Eli the priest hears the petition of Hannah and gives her a blessing:

> *Go in peace; the God of Israel grant the petition you have made to him.* (1 Samuel 1:17)

In due course Hannah becomes pregnant and keeps her promise that her son should be given to YHWH:

> *For this child I prayed; and the Lord has granted me the petition that I made to him. Therefore I have lent him to the Lord; as long as he lives, he is given to the Lord.* (1 Samuel 1:27–28)

In response to the birth and dedication of her son, Hannah offers an exuberant doxology to God (1 Samuel 2:1–10). She does not sing of her son; rather, she sings of the transformative, disruptive, revolutionary power of YHWH as she anticipates the king to come (v. 10).

Early on, the boy, Samuel ("asked of the Lord"), was assigned to work at the local sanctuary of Shiloh (2:19–3:1). The final episode in Samuel's formation concerns his dramatic encounter with the God of whom Hannah has sung (I Samuel 3:1-19). Without explanation or embarrassment, the narrative reports the way in which YHWH, in the night, summoned Samuel:

> *Samuel, Samuel.* (3:4)

The boy thought it was the priest, Eli, calling him. The Lord called him again:

> *Samuel!* (3:6)

By the call the third time, Eli has figured out the voice addressing Samuel:

> *Go, lie down; and if he calls you, you shall say, "Speak Lord, for your servant is listening."* (v. 9)

Now a fourth time:

> *Samuel, Samuel.* (v. 10)

This time the connection is made; Samuel answers as Eli has instructed him. The connection is made, even though the news delivered is not good for Eli and his priestly family (vv. 11–14). The narrative thus concerns Samuel's growth into his demanding vocation:

> *As Samuel grew up, the Lord was with him and let none of his words fall to the ground.* (3:19)

What interests us here is that Eli bet on Samuel. He did all the prep work with the boy so that he could be responsive to his vocation. In the end, Eli does not flinch from the hard words given to Samuel concerning his house (3:18). Thus, day by day in the sanctuary, Eli nurtured and guided Samuel to be ready for this moment that would ignite his life. It is impossible to imagine the boy coming to his vocation without Eli's good, reliable bet. Most often, when we read this narrative, we stop at 3:10 with Samuel's ready response to the summons of God. Beyond that, the narrative becomes less favorable and more demanding. The less familiar part of Samuel's story, lacking in such brilliant idyllic charm, follows. At the outset Samuel functions to continue the line of "judges" featured in the book of Judges. He calls for repentance, offers sacrifices, and mobilizes Israel to defeat the Philistines (1 Samuel 7:3–16). At the end of this report, he "administers justice" (7:17).

By chapter 8 Samuel is confronted with a great crisis. He is a representative and embodiment of the old order of the judges. But now popular opinion in Israel demands a king, thus rejecting the old order of the judges in order to replicate the practice of other nations

(1 Samuel 8:4–18). After Samuel resists and refuses such popular opinion, he is instructed by YHWH to give in to the demand for a king (8:22). This is against Samuel's better judgment and apparently against the better judgment of YHWH as well.

We may identify three subsequent moments in Samuel's career. First, after the failure of Saul as king, Samuel once more performs his role as judge (1 Samuel 12:1–23). His reperformance consists in three parts:

(a) He offers a statement of his own rectitude so that he can legitimately continue his leadership role:

> *Here I am; testify against me before the Lord and before his anointed. Whose ox have I taken? Or whose donkey have I taken? Or whom have I defrauded? Whom have I oppressed? Or from whose hand have I taken a bribe to blind my eyes with it? Testify against me and I will restore it to you.* (1 Samuel 12:3)

The people readily acquit him.

(b) Samuel offers a review of YHWH's "saving deeds" upon which Israel may continue to rely:

> *Now therefore take your stand, so that I may enter into judgment with you before the Lord, and I will declare to you all the saving deeds of the Lord that he performed for you and for your ancestors.* (v. 7)

It is as though he insists that the old order is sufficient for the life and well-being of Israel.

(c) In his role as judge Samuel offers guidance to his people with a summons to "fear and serve" YHWH and an assurance to the people that YHWH has not and will not reject Israel (12:20–24). This chapter is like a "last stand" for the old order of judges that Samuel has so faithfully and effectively enacted.

But then the narrative abruptly shifts gears. Samuel, who has resisted kingship and rejected Saul, now becomes a willing king-maker. He is led to Bethlehem, where he sees and surveys the sons of Jesse. He is readily drawn to Jesse's handsome, attractive sons as candidates for kingship, but finally he gets it right. He settles on the youngest, least noticed son of Jesse:

> *The Lord said, "Rise and anoint him; for this is the one." Then Samuel took the horn of oil, and anointed him in the presence of his brothers; and the spirit of the Lord came mightily upon David from that day forward. Samuel then set out and went to Ramah.* (1 Samuel 16:12–13)

Samuel has completed his work in making Israel's transition to monarchy. And then he died:

> *Now Samuel died; and all Israel assembled and mourned for him. They buried him at his home in Ramah.* (1 Samuel 25:1)

I have wondered: did Samuel remember Eli as he resisted kingship? Did he think of Eli as he reasserted his role as judge? Did he think of Eli as he became a knowing king-maker at Bethlehem? We do not know. But Eli sure is engrained in him whether he was aware of it or not. He had been formed for this work, and he did not try to escape from the destiny into which Eli had initiated him.

We might have expected that this report of his death would be the final notice of Samuel in the narrative. But Samuel lingers (1 Samuel 28:15–19). In death he is "brought up" to dispute Saul again. In his death-marked speech to fearful Saul, Samuel confirms the rejection of Saul and YHWH's designation of David as king:

> *The Lord has done to you just as he spoke by me; for the Lord has torn the kingdom out of your hand, and given it to your neighbor, David.* (1 Samuel 28:17)

In that utterance, Samuel opens the way for the rule of David and the long narrative account of the dynasty of David that will eventually end in exile (I and II Kings). Samuel is this remarkable figure who presides over the decisive transformation of Israel from a tribal society to a monarchy. He is reluctant to make that move, but is swept along by the irresistible drive of David, who is recognized here to be propelled by divine intention in the form and force of the Spirit.

It is never easy to see the adult in the child. But the child on whom Eli had bet turns out to be the adult who was most required in Israel. We may conclude that all that happened in the adult life of Samuel was seeded and evoked in inchoate form in the child. Samuel had been bet on by his mother, Hannah. Samuel had been bet on by the priest, Eli. Together they fashioned an identity and a calling for the boy. In the end, it is unmistakably clear that YHWH had bet on Samuel. But YHWH's bet only came to fruition by way of Hannah and Eli, mother and priest. The fruition of such an adult can only happen via human bets. Like Holmes with his law clerks and like Frankfurter with his law students, Hannah and Eli did the betting that produced this remarkable adult who carried in his body the force of his faith (the faith of Israel) into the public domain of Israel.

It occurs to me that the church is a community properly engaged in betting on children and young people. Many others will teach children the way to "succeed" or "do well" or "make a good living." But the evocation of adults with sustainable character is peculiar work of the synagogue and the church upon which the future of our democratic society depends. Thus, a congregation is an arena for such a bet.

In the congregation every child is known by name—every child, not only the "bright and beautiful." Every child is identified by name and supported in love and empowered to live in covenantal fidelity. Surely it is the case that baptism is the act whereby the church sacramentally bets on a child. And confirmation is the glad awareness by the young person that "I have been bet on!" Such "betting" is a day-to-day thing. It is done in community, but it is a one-at-a-time act for the child. It is work that requires patience and attentiveness of a daily kind. The bet cannot be rushed, and the child, to be sure, exercises great freedom in how to live out that bet.

There is one other note to mark concerning Eli. He had failed quite miserably with his own sons (1 Samuel 2:22–25, 27–34). Given his sorry failure as a parent, Eli nevertheless is empowered and authorized to be the one who would effectively bet on Samuel. It is not hard to imagine that Samuel inhaled the good words of Eli and that these words helped to shape this adult who was given courage and resolve for his dangerous, obedient life.

At least in the Gospel of Luke there is no doubt that Jesus's early life is narrated in a way that is patterned after the life of Samuel as a boy. Thus, in her "Magnificat," mother Mary reiterates the Song of Hannah (Luke 1:46–53; see 1 Samuel 2:1–10). Luke, moreover, in his report on Jesus as a boy, can write:

> *The child grew and became strong, filled with wisdom; and the favor of God was upon him.* (Luke 2:40)

The words are an echo of 1 Samuel 2:29. In due course not only mother Mary and the shepherds (Luke 2:8–20), Simeon (Luke 2:25–35), and Anna (Luke 2:36–38) all bet on Jesus. Before Luke finishes his narrative of the child, he will exclaim that *God bet on Jesus* at his baptism:

> *And a voice came from heaven, "You are my Son, the Beloved; with you I am well pleased."* (Luke 3:22)

God bet on Jesus:

> *The Spirit of the Lord is upon me,*
> *because he has anointed me to bring good news to the poor.*
> *He has sent me to proclaim release to the captives*
> *and recovery of sight to the blind,*
> *to let the oppressed go free,*
> *to proclaim the year of the Lord's favor.* (Luke 4:18–19)

God bet on Jesus to live a transformative life in the world among the needy. *God bet on Jesus* to sustain his obedience all the way to Friday, not to flinch before the powers who would finally execute him. *God bet on Jesus* early Sunday to initiate the new age of resurrection. In the church's mumbling, long-term effort to articulate the mystery of "Incarnation and Trinity," our attempt is to show how it is that God bet on Jesus, the way a Father would bet on a Son.

It follows, does it not, that as God bet on Jesus, so *God bets on the people of Jesus,*

> to do the transformative work for the disinherited,
> to engage in risky obedience, and
> to sign on for life in the new age of love and justice,
> righteousness, and compassion.

Imagine what it is like, in our "dark night," to ponder the mystery that we have been bet on by the God who does not flinch from very long odds.

11

START WITH ME TOO

A LONG TIME ago, I read *The Secret of Santa Vittori* (1966) by Robert Crichton. I recently reread it. It is a wonderful novel about a back-country peasant community in Italy during World War II. This village of peasants is an out-of-the-way place disconnected from the larger social reality and only wants to be left alone. It is very poor; its one claim to pride and well-being is producing wonderful wine in great quantities. The story revolves around a small regiment of German-Nazi soldiers who come to confiscate the great wine supplies of the village, while the villagers are fully determined to hide the wine and refuse to yield it to the Germans. The small cadre of German soldiers tries for a long time to befriend the villagers and discover the hidden wine. But the villagers are sly and wily and refuse to give in.

The story turns when the Germans lose their patience with the clever peasants and send in SS agents who resort to violence and torture to discover the wine. They try to break the silence of the peasants who refuse to reveal the location of the wine. The peasants suffer greatly but continue to decline to tell the Germans. Ultimately, the Germans are frustrated and depart, leaving the village greatly wounded, but with its dignity and wine intact. One at a time, the lead characters in the novel, under great duress, refuse.

In a summary retrospective, Crichton's narrator observes:

> *The truth is this: If only one man among all of the rest will not break, as Fabio and then Cavalcanti did not break, then all of them, all those who so despise men that they believe all men can be broken and all men can be bought,* all *of them have*

> *failed and all of them are defeated, because one alone destroys them and one alone can give heart to all other men.* (356)

This final sentence here caught my attention:

> *One alone can give heart to all other men.*

Bravery and faithfulness are contagious! The narrator continues:

> *So, no matter whatever else happens here, we have this reason at least to be proud. Man is an animal, but he doesn't have to end as one. Perhaps this is the lesson the Germans never succeeded in learning.* (256–257)

The courage and faithfulness of the few saved the wine, the dignity of the village, and the well-being of the people.

These remarkable lines in the novel evoked two responses from me. First, it recalled to me a favorite song of the "boys' choir" of our wee high school that the choir loved to sing and we loved to hear. The lines are from *The New Moon*, a romantic operetta of Sigmund Romberg in 1930 with the lyrics by Oscar Hammerstein:

> *Give me ten men who are stout-hearted men*
> *who will fight for the right they adore.*
> *Start me with ten who are stout-hearted men*
> *and I'll soon give you ten thousand more.*
> *Shoulder to shoulder, and bolder and bolder*
> *they grow as they go to the fore.*
> *Then there's nothing in the world*
> *can halt or mar a plan*
> *when stout-hearted men*
> *Come together man-to-man.*

We had no idea about the plot of the operetta, trite as it is. What mattered to us was the image of strong, brave men and boys attracting other strong, brave men and boys to the song and to the walk.

A second, more important thought, after the narrative of Santa Vittoria, is the Israelite narrative of two brave leaders, Joshua and Caleb. Dennis Olson's *The Death of the Old and the Birth of the New: The Framework of the Book of Numbers and the Pentateuch* (1985) has traced, with singular clarity, the narrative function of Joshua and Caleb in the memory of Israel. Olson shows how, after Moses, the faithful leadership of Israel is reduced to the faithfulness of these two, and only these two. The textual evidence abounds. When the land of promise is spied out by Israel, they learn that it is a good, prosperous, productive land. The mass of Israelites were afraid of the inhabitants of the land. It is first Caleb who is eager to enter the land of promise (Numbers 13:30). In the face of fearful resistance, it is Joshua and Caleb who refuse the fearfulness of their company:

> *And Joshua son of Nun and Caleb son Jephunneh, who were among those who had spied out the land, tore their clothes and said to all the congregation of the Israelites, "The land that we went through as spies is an exceedingly good land. If the Lord is pleased with us, he will bring us into this land and give it to us, a land that flows with milk and honey. Only, do not rebel against the Lord; and do not fear the people of the land, for they are no more than bread for us; their protection is removed from them, and the Lord is with us; do not fear them."* (Numbers 14:6–9)

Moses recognizes that the two of them are exceptional in Israel:

> *Not one of you shall come into the land in which I swore to settle you, except Caleb son of Jephunneh and Joshua son of Nun.* (14:30)

Eventually all the doubters died.

> *But Joshua son of Nun and Caleb son of Jephunneh alone remained alive, of those men who went to spy out the land.* (v. 38)

The point is confirmed later in the book of Numbers:

> *Not one of them was left, except Caleb son of Jephunneh and Joshua son of Nun.* (26:65)

They are the two who have "unreservedly followed the Lord" (32:12).

While the venture of Numbers 14 was foiled, the thread of faithfulness by the two endures into the land entry.

> *Not one of these—not one of this evil generation—shall see the good land that I swore to give to your ancestors, except Caleb son of Jephunneh. He shall see it, and to him and to his descendants I will give the land on which he set foot, because of his complete fidelity to the Lord. Even with me the Lord was angry on your account, saying, "You shall not enter there. Joshua son of Nun, your assistant, shall enter there; encourage him, for he is the one who will secure Israel's possession of it."* (Deuteronomy 1:35–38)

The singularity of the two is confirmed in the narrative account of land settlement. In Joshua 14:6–12 Caleb offers a speech of self-justification as the ground on which he should receive a portion of the land of promise. He reiterates his uncompromised fidelity and reminds that YHWH had promised him land. And then:

> *Joshua blessed him, and gave Hebron to Caleb son of Jephunneh for an inheritance. So Hebron became the*

> *inheritance of Caleb son of Jephunneh the Kenizzite to this day, because he wholeheartedly followed the Lord, the God of Israel.* (Joshua 14:13–14)

The bestowal of Hebron to Caleb is confirmed in Joshua 15:13 and Judges 1:20.

This extended, complex narrative is as though Moses had said, "Give me two men." Start me with only two. Only these two, Joshua and Celeb, were required for the narrative to reach its fulfillment. No others are listed as consistently faithful to the will of YHWH or to the destiny of Israel. But the two are enough. It is enough to have two leaders who are devoted to the promises of YHWH and who will run the risks that inescapably accompany the promises. Thus, the two become the link and carrier of covenantal promises and covenantal requirements of YHWH into the land of Canaan.

Faithfulness as the practice of risk and danger is the story of *a few good women and men.* In Santa Vittoria it was *one such man at a time,* though there were many in sequence. In the operetta, it was *ten stout-hearted men.* And in ancient Israel, two faithful men kept the promise—and the community—alive into the good land.

We may draw several lessons from this story of one at a time in Santa Vittoria, ten in the operetta, and two in ancient Israel:

1. A few brave, good people can make a decisive difference and alter history. Thus, in the novel, the wine and the dignity of the peasant village are saved, not least by Babbaluche, the cobbler, who was selected as a hostage to be executed, not least by Joshua and Caleb who bravely led their companions on a risky mission.
2. The bravery of a few good people is a magnetic force that will draw others to it, because many well-intentioned people are not brave, but can follow if led.

3. The brave work of the few is never the work of an isolated individual, even if done alone. In the case of those who suffered mightily, one at a time in the novel, they did so in the village's resolved, unwavering company. Joshua and Caleb ran their risks of faithfulness because they understood that the community had risks to run to receive the promises.

Our society is at a critical historical juncture that requires a few good women and men. The wealth gap between rich and poor grows, the rendition of vulnerable people as commodities places the human community in deep jeopardy, and the environment spoils the health of creation. The wealthy, who benefit from and enjoy the wealth gap and the managers and beneficiaries of privatized prosperity, the powerful who exploit the poor, and those who produce the poison of our planet count on the rest of us to be compliant, even if in dissent. The spell of such fearful compliance can be and will be broken only by the few good women and men who dare to march to a different drummer, work from a different script, and act in ways congruent with their conviction of a world held in the good hands of the creator.

Those who make such a move may hear it this way:

Start me with ten . . . as in the operetta!
Start me with two . . . as in ancient Israel!
Start me with one . . . as at Santa Vittoria!

Start locally in the neighborhood. Start in a way that references covenantal norms of reality.

This covenantal version of reality was offered in Israel at length in the narrative concerning those who spied out the land:

We came to the land to which you sent us; it flows with milk and honey, and this [grapes, pomegranates, figs] is its

> *fruit. Yet the people who live in the land are strong, and the towns are fortified and very large; and besides, we saw the descendants of Anak there. The Amalekites live in the land of the Negeb; the Hittites, the Jebusites, and the Amorites live in the hill country; and the Canaanites live by the sea, and along the Jordan.* (Numbers 13:27–29)

Immediately Caleb counters such an opinion:

> *Let us go up at once and occupy it, for we are well able to overcome it.* (v. 30)

But the frightened ones are insistent:

> *We are not able to go up against this people, for they are stronger than we . . . The land that we have gone through as spies is a land that devours its inhabitants; and all the people that we see in it are of great size. There we saw the Nephilim (the Anakites come from the Nephilim); and to ourselves we seemed like grasshoppers, and so we seemed to them.* (vv. 31–33)

Their despair permeates the community:

> *Then all the congregation raised a loud cry, and the people wept that night. And all the Israelites complained against Moses and Aaron; the whole congregation said to them, "Would that we had died in the land of Egypt! Or would that we had died in this wilderness! Why is the Lord bringing us into this land to fall by the sword? Our wives and our little ones will become booty; would it not be better for us to go back to Egypt?" So they said to one another, "Let us choose a captain, and go back to Egypt."* (Numbers 14:1–4)

Again, the two brave ones speak up in response:

> *The Lord is with us; do not fear them.* (14:9)

The narrative is long, complex, and unresolved. But finally all that generation that held back in fear had died:

> *The men who brought an unfavorable report about the land died by a plague before the Lord.* (Numbers 14:37)

Joshua and Caleb, the brave ones, prevailed:

> *But Joshua son of Nun and Caleb son of Jephunneh alone remained alive, of those men who went to spy out the land.* (v. 38)

This narrative plot is often reperformed, wherever a few good women and men act for a better, altered future. It could happen even among us!

12

THE RESULTS MEN

IN HER BOOK, *Legacy of Violence: A History of the British Empire* (2022), Caroline Elkins details the predatory way of the British Empire amid its colonies. The Empire existed precisely to effect the extraction from the colonies of cheap labor and cheap material resources needed by Britain. The maintenance and administration of the extraction domain of the Empire was led by a series of bureaucratic governors-general and their aides, whose work was to maintain the orderly processes of extraction while at the same time maintaining a facade of civility. Among the bureaucratic administrators Elkins names in particular are Terence Gavaghan, Gerald Templer, and Orde Wingate. What caught my eye is that Elkins labels these several colonial administrators as "results men," that is, as servants of the Empire who were particularly interested in and committed to "results" and who had no scruples about the means required to achieve desired results (p. 575). Those means included any form of violence necessary to achieve the "results."

The phrase "results men" got me thinking: perhaps every empire relies eventually on "results men." Thus, Henry VIII had Thomas Cromwell (on which see the trilogy of Hilary Putnam), and Richard Nixon famously had Bob Haldeman and John Ehrlichman. And even George Washington had Alexander Hamilton and Franklin Roosevelt had Sydney Hillman.

Pushing back behind such instances, I had the thought that the primary nominee in the Bible for a "result man" would most likely be Joab, the great ruthless military man who did the dirty work to support the rise of David to kingship. The narrative of 2 Samuel, our primary "historical" source for David, is much preoccupied with the actions of

Joab. Joab was even above the "mighty men of David" (2 Samuel 23:8–37); in the formation of David's inchoate royal government Joab was "over the army," that is, Secretary of Defense or Chief of Staff (8:16, 20:23). He earned his way to that latter post with David by his courage and bravery, and by his unfailing, uncompromising loyalty to David. In passing, we are told that Joab won great military victories for David against the Arameans and the Moabites (2 Samuel 10:7–14). Not only does he defeat the Ammonites, but at exactly the right moment, he defers to David, summoning David to come to claim the victory that Joab has won for him:

> *Joab sent messengers to David, and said, "I have fought against Rabbah; moreover, I have taken the water city. Now, then, gather the rest of the people together, and encamp against the city, and take it; or I myself will take the city, and it will be called by my name." So David gathered all the people together and went to Rabbah, and fought against it, and took it. He took the crown of Milcom from his head; the weight of it was a talent of gold, and in it was a precious stone; and it was placed on David's head. He also brought forth the spoil of the city, a very great amount.* (2 Samuel 12:27–30).

More important for our purpose than these battle reports are the specific narrative accounts of Joab's hand-to-hand performance, partly in loyalty to David, partly in revenge, and partly to secure his own position. We may identify five such moments in Joab's military career.

1. At the outset, David is at war with Saul for the throne. A subplot is the rivalry of two military families, Abner in the north and Joab and his brothers, sons of Zeruiah, in the South. In their bitter struggle for preeminence, Abner seeks to avoid the killing of Joab's brother Ahasel, but Ahasel foolishly persists and is killed by Abner (2:18–23).

In the next paragraph, Abner talks Joab down from more violence (2:26–28). But soon, the conflict between David and Saul continues. Saul's general, Abner, seeks peace terms with David (3:9–21). David turns down Abner's conciliatory (likely self-serving) move, but Joab rightly sees Abner as his rival for leadership. As quickly as he can, Joab stabs Abner to death as service to David and to advance his own interest (3:26–28). While Abner's death may have benefitted David, David cannot afford to be identified with the killing. For that reason, he publicly humiliates Joab (3:31), while he himself conspicuously grieved for the slain Abner (3:32–37). He asserts his own innocence in a masterful public relations act and voices his deep resentment concerning Joab and his brothers:

> *Today I am powerless, even though the anointed king; these men, the sons of Zeruiah, are too violent for me.* (2 Samuel 3:39)

The narrative has provided a clue for us about the jeopardy already building against Joab and his brothers.

2. But Joab is unfazed in his utter loyalty to David. He leads David's battle against the Moabites while David remains at home (2 Samuel 11:1). And then Joab silently, but with full understanding, undertakes the elimination of Uriah the Hittite, so as to eliminate an acute embarrassment for David. Indeed, Joab not only silently acts out David's wish for the elimination of Uriah (11:16–17) but takes great care to formulate his report to David with the wink of an eye:

> *The men gained an advantage over us, and came out against us in the field; but we drove them back to the entrance of the gate. Then the archers shot at your servants from the wall; some of the king's servants are dead; and your servant Uriah the Hittite is dead also.* (2 Samuel 11:23–24)

Joab understands everything and says nothing. David nicely reassures Joab; all the while the two men have a silent agreement about what they have done together (11:25). Joab is fully implicated in the killing by David, or conversely, David is fully implicated in the killing by Joab. Either way, they have colluded in killing that served David well.

3. Joab asserts himself into the complex relationship between David and his son, Absalom (14:1–20). Joab acts, we are told, because he knows that Absalom was "on the king's heart" (v. 1). Through a complex stratagem Joab manages to get Absalom fully and honorably readmitted to the king's presence (14:31). And then, by the very next verse, Absalom acts the rebel who wishes to seize the throne from his father (2 Samuel; 15:1–12). While Joab has acted to restore Absalom to royal favor, there is no ambiguity about Joab's loyalty. He is all David! Consequently, after such a treasonable initiative, elaborate negotiations, and conflict between father and son, the settlement of the rebellion all comes down to Joab's action. Joab is a "results man." He does not hesitate to act. Absalom may be a beloved son of the king, but Joab reckons him to be a traitor to his father. Joab has no patience for such niceties as the king's emotion:

> *I will not waste time like this with you. He took three spears in his hand, and thrust them into the heart of Absalom, while he was still alive in the oak. And ten young men, Joab's armor-bearers, surrounded Absalom and struck him, and killed him.* (2 Samuel 18:14–15)

Joab has produced a result for his king. The rebel is dead.

Joab did what he had to do without blinking. He knows that the news of Absalom's death will not go down well with the king. And so, as in the case of the report of the death of Uriah the Hittite, Joab takes care about his communication with the king. To protect a well-connected messenger, Ahimaaz, son of Zadok the priest, Joab shrewdly dispatches a different messenger, a foreigner, a nameless Cushite (18:19–21). And of course, the news of the death of Absalom, the traitor-son, does not go well with the king. Now, for the first time, David names Absalom as "my son":

> *O my son, Absalom, my son, my son Absalom! Would I had died instead of you, O Absalom, my son, my son! . . . O my son Absalom, O Absalom, my son, my son!* (2 Samuel 18:33, 19:4)

The "results man" is undeterred by the grief of the king. He has a throne to worry about with no time for a weeping father. He rebukes the king for his public show of grief:

> *Then Joab came to the house of the king, and said, "Today you have covered with shame the faces of all your officers who have saved your life today, and the lives of your sons and your daughters, and the lives of your wives and your concubines, for love of those who hate you and for hatred of those who love you. You have made it clear today that commanders and officers are nothing to you; for I perceive that if Absalom were alive and all of us were dead today, then you would be pleased. So go out at once and speak kindly to your servants; for I swear by the Lord, if you do not go, not a man will stay with you this night; and this will be worse for you than any disaster that has come upon you from your youth until now."* (2 Samuel 19:5–8)

Joab *commands* the king to make a public appearance, to wave to the crowd in triumph, or he will lose public support. The king *obeys* the uncompromising man of results!

Then the king got up and took his seat in the gate. The troops were all told, "See, the king is sitting in the gate," and all the troops came before the king (2 Samuel 19:8).

4. We now have three "results" that Joab has worked on behalf of David:

- the elimination of Abner,
- the elimination of Uriah, and
- the elimination of Absalom.

Joab's action against Abner grated upon the king. David relied on Joab for the death of Uriah. In the case of Absalom, the king says nothing to Joab, but he surely was troubled by the death. But David's vexation with Joab was not yet acute. And now, in a fourth case that is much less complex, Joab secures another "result" for his king. He confronts the rebellion of Sheba, who leads a now feeble remnant of Saul's following. Joab negotiates the death of Sheba, the rebel:

> *Then the woman went to all the people with her wise plan. And they cut off the head of Sheba son of Bichri, and threw it out to Joab. So he blew the trumpet, and they dispersed from the city, and all went to their homes, while Joab returned to Jerusalem to the king.* (2 Samuel 20:22)

The matter receives no commentary, but David's throne is again made secure.

5. Finally, we have one other episode in which Joab acts for the king, albeit this time against his own better judgment. The king proposes to conduct a census of "the people of Israel and Judah" (24:l). Joab knows that a census smacks of the bureaucracy of a kingdom that can serve only for taxation or a military draft, neither of which could be a popular enterprise. Joab puts a question to the king:

> *But why does my lord the king want to do this?* (24:3)

He poses the question, but it is not really a question. It is a rebuke to the king, like, "Why would you do such a stupid thing?" He warns the king against a mistaken policy initiative. David, however, is unyielding:

> *But the king's word prevailed against Joab and the army commanders.* (v. 4)

Having raised his objection to the king, Joab now acts in full and prompt obedience and initiates the king's wish:

> *So Joab and the commanders of the army went out from the presence of the king to take a census of the people of Israel. They crossed the Jordan, and began from Aroer and from the city that is in the middle of the valley, toward Gad and on to Jazer. Then they came to Gilead, and to Kadesh in the land of the Hittites; and they came to Dan, and from Dan they went around to Sidon, and came to the fortress of Tyre, and to all the cities of the Hivites and Canaanites; and they went out to the Negeb of Judah at Beersheba. So when they had gone all through the land, they came back to Jerusalem at the end of nine months and twenty days. Joab reported to the king the number of those who had been recorded: in Israel there were eight hundred thousand soldiers able to draw the sword, and those of Judah were five hundred thousand.* (2 Samuel 24:4–9).

We notice that the military conducts the census, and the outcome of the census is the number of potential soldiers. Thus, the census aims to determine the extent of David's military capacity.

Of course, we learn promptly at 24:10 that Joab had been right at the outset:

> *But afterward, David was stricken to the heart because he had numbered the people. David said to the Lord, "I have sinned greatly in what I have done . . ."* (2 Samuel 24:10)

Joab had obeyed his king, but he had yet again crossed the king's will. There is no future comment on the matter.

We are not surprised by the turn of the narrative against Joab. Like all "men of results," this one in ancient Israel is expendable. Joab has been steadfast in his intense loyalty to David. He has acted regularly in the king's interest. Even so, Joab's actions rubbed against the will of the king. He had killed Abner when David wanted Abner as an ally. He had killed Absalom, who was David's well-beloved son. He contradicted the king concerning the census. David arrives in the narrative when "enough is enough." And so, after the narrative concerning Absalom, David, who had fled from Jerusalem, is impatient about his return to his city; he is eager to be restored (19:9–10). He sends a chiding word to his two priests, Zadok and Abiathar; he reminds them that they are family (20:11–12). And then abruptly this:

> *And say to Amasa, "Are you not my bone and my flesh? So may God do to me, and more, if you are not the commander of my army from now on, in place of Joab." Amasa swayed the hearts of all the people of Judah as one, and they sent word to the king, "Return, both you and all your servants." So the king came back to the Jordan, and Judah came to Gilgal to meet the king and bring him over the Jordan.*
> (2 Samuel 19:13–15)

The narrative had not apprised us of when the king deposed Joab without explanation. David finds Amasa a useful figure who presides over his triumphant return to Jerusalem. Joab has been "fired." (This must have shocked the public, not unlike President Truman's dismissal of General McArthur!) Joab is gone in a whiff because, his many results withstanding, he has been around too long, has so many detractors, and is now eagerly swept away. Thus, it is with many "result men," like Cromwell, Haldeman, and Ehrlichman. They are useful, and then they are used up. And so David, who makes his triumphant return to the city, amid much jubilation, alongside his new commander in his company. Of course, many rushed to greet the king, hoping to find favor from him. Among those who gushed over the returning king was Shimei, who had been previously saved by David, even though he had cursed the king (2 Samuel 16:5–14). Some thought Shimei should die for such cursing. Among those who believed that was Abishai, brother of Joab:

> *Abishai, son of Zeruiah answered, "Shall not Shimei be put to death for this, because he cursed the Lord's anointed?"* (2 Samuel 19:21)

The king responds with what is now a refrain (see 3:39):

> *What have I to do with you, you sons of Zeruiah, that you should become an adversary to me today?* (2 Samuel 19:22)

And so Shimei is spared, perhaps to spite Joab and his family. No mention is made of Joab. Indeed, no need of Joab for the restoration of David. The king, as kings do, has moved on, and Joab is used up without thanks and pity.

But Joab is now so filled with resentment that he acts abruptly to eliminate the man, Amasa, who has replaced him in favor of David:

> *And Joab took Amasa by the beard with his right hand to kiss him. But Amasa did not notice the sword in Joab's hand; Joab struck him in the belly so that his entrails poured out on the ground, and he died. He did not strike a second blow.* (2 Samuel 20:9–10)

This ending is like what we might expect from a man of results who now is an enemy of the king and of the king's new commander:

> *Amasa lay wallowing in his blood on the highway, and the man [one of Joab's men] saw that all the people were stopping. Since he saw that all who came by were stopping, he carried Amasa from the highway into a field, and threw a garment over him. Once he was removed from the highway, all the people went on after Joab to pursue Sheba son of Bichri.*
> (2 Samuel 19:12–13)

It is as though Joab was able to retain some of his popular support, at least for a time. That popular support, however, counted for nothing when the king had decided otherwise.

Finally, we come to the tricky moment when David must transfer power to his son. By now, Joab is a spent force. But he is still around, and now he sides with David's son, Adonijah, in the contest for succession (1 Kings 1:7). But Joab, now disregarded and forgotten, has his political judgment fail him. He bets on the wrong son! He sided with Adonijah and not Solomon, the son of Bathsheba. It is her son who will become king.

It remains only to give sad closure to the life and work of Joab, the consummate "result man." David had long been uneasy about Joab and his brothers and their violent propensity. He was uneasy even though their violence mostly had been in his service. Thus, it is not a great surprise that in the drawn-out deathbed scene of the old king, Joab's name comes up once more. In 1 Kings 2:1–4, David issues his last counsel to his successor, his son Solomon. These lines must have been for public consumption to exhibit the old king as a worthy son of the Torah. What follows this paragraph is a very different kind of advice for the new king, surely not intended for the public. In verses 5–9, we go behind the public portrayal of the king and actually see how "royal sausage" is made. These verses show that the old king (or the narrator) has a long, unforgiving memory. There is one happy note in these hard verses, a generous remembrance of Barzillai, on which see 2 Samuel 19:31–40 and 1 Kings 2:7. Otherwise, the king's words are about settling old scores. On the one hand, there is a death sentence for Shimei, the northern rebel whom David had let live, perhaps to spite Joab (2:8–9). On the other hand, there is Joab, who comes first on the list of the king:

> *Moreover you know also what Joab son of Zeruiah did to me, how he dealt with the two commanders of the armies of Israel, Abner son of Ner, and Amasa son of Jether, whom he murdered, retaliating in time of peace for blood that had been shed in war, and putting the blood of war on the belt around his waist, and on the sandals of his feet. Act therefore according to your wisdom, but do not let his gray head go down to Sheol in peace.* (2 Kings 2:5–6)

He issues a death sentence for his best "result man." He has no ambiguity about the matter. He has no more use for the ruthlessness of Joab.

Solomon is quick to act. First he deals with his rival brother, Adonijah (vv. 13–25). His agent in the execution is Benaniah, who has replaced Joab as military commander. Second, there is Abiathar, the priest who also bet on the wrong son (see 1:7). Respecting his sacral office, Abiathar is banned and not executed "at this time" (2:26–27). Third, there is Joab (vv. 28–30). The killing of Joab is carefully done. Benaniah, the new "result man," sends word back to Solomon and receives assurance before he acts. But Solomon is adamant and unwavering; he can recall the same two killings by Joab that his father had named:

> *He attacked and killed with the sword two men more righteous and better than himself, Abner son of Ner, commander of the army of Israel, and Amasa son of Jether, commander of the army of Judah.* (1 Kings 2:32)

Joab is now a pitiful figure grasping at the horns of the altar. Now he has no more medals, no more rank, and no more prestige. He is desperate, but his belated appeal to the Lord of altar and tent do him no good now. It is too late; he dies as result men are wont to do, unwept, unmissed, ungrieved. And Benaiah is now secure in his office. To conclude the paragraph, Shimei gets the same fate, even though David had let him live (2:36–46). It only required these several deaths to settle old scores and to secure the throne:

> *So the kingdom was established in the hand of Solomon.*
> (1 Kings 2:46)

The kingdom of David had no more lasting commitment to this result man than did the British Empire. We are left to wonder why some willingly take on the role of "result men." And why we engage them to do that work. The "results" often do not pan out. And we wonder, in the wake of this violence, if there could be "a more excellent way."

When the church reads the narrative of Joab, it can reflect upon the need for and the problem of "result" women and men. The church is not a natural habitat for "result men" or women. No doubt, the church requires few such people in its midst because there are plans to be made, decisions to be faced, buildings to be maintained, budgets to be managed, and programs to be implemented. There is a need for some "results" in the church. For the most part, however, the church is not a community designed for or called to results. It is a movement of glad people "on the way" with Jesus. That journey is a meandering path with Jesus, from village to village, from hurt to hurt, from need to need, and from hope to hope. Thus, as every wise pastor knows, the real "business" of most church meetings is not "the business," but the richness of interaction among the members in a process that my friend, John McKnight, terms "associational life." The church is a company in which, in a face-to-face way,

> *If one member suffers, all suffer together; if one is honored, all rejoice.* (1 Corinthians 12:26)

In the process of such neighboring, the church obeys the gospel to do the reconciling, emancipatory, transformative work of Jesus. It is a way of life not propelled by "results" but by *faithfulness*. Therefore, the church starkly contrasts every "empire" and every agency driven by "results." Given such a different mandate, we are "on the way," a way that may be as joyous as it may be costly.

13

THE FUNDAMENTAL DILEMMA

WITH FEW EXCEPTIONS, most of us in mainline (old line) Protestantism arrive at church carrying a deep and unacknowledged ambiguity. (I think it is the same for others beyond such Protestantism who arrive at church.) We arrive at church to pray and sing because we do indeed treasure the gospel as the truth of our lives. At the same time, we arrive at church with deep images pressed into our imagination concerning US exceptionalism, racial superiority, and economic expectations for success. This ambiguity requires preachers to tread carefully, lest the ambiguity be rawly exposed. This task is even more delicate since the preacher usually carries the same ambiguity in their life. This ambiguity is our contemporary form of the old "Halfway Covenant" that the Puritans devised in 1662 to make room in the church for the "baptized but unconverted" parents to have their children baptized. It was a way of allowing into the church those who were nominally committed to the gospel but who were able to hold back from the faith with reservations based on other grounds. The Halfway Covenant (and our widespread ambiguity) makes the church and its worship an unsettled, uneasy proposition that can be sorted out only with care, honesty, and passion. My purpose here is to consider that ambiguity that sits at the heart of the church as it gathers.

I was alerted to this implicit but mostly unacknowledged reality by reading *The Enchantments of Mammon: How Capitalism became the Religion of Modernity* (2019) by Eugene McCarraher. In articulating this "fundamental dilemma," McCarraher asserts:

> *The gradual demise of the Puritan social gospel was witness to the fundamental dilemma of the elect: their quest for a*

> *beloved community built on the foundations of capitalist enterprise. They resolved the dilemma with a covenant theology of capitalism, a creed whose doctrinal elements included the affirmation of wealth as a divine appointment; territorial conquest to enlarge the parameters of God's rich and faithful metropolis; a conception of the natural world as a providential storehouse of vendable wonders; and a jeremiad tradition to chastise moral failing and obscure the intractable persistence of the dilemma.* (117)

McCarraher suggests four components to this dilemma: I suggest there are four acute accent points in our articulation of the gospel that require sustained pastoral consideration if the church is to be freed for missional energy and missional engagement.

1. The affirmation of wealth as a divine appointment. The Book of Proverbs readily attests that God blesses the rich as those who are in sync with the creator and the ordering of creation:

> *A slack hand cause poverty,*
> *but the hand of the diligent makes rich.* (Proverbs 10:4)
>
> *The blessing of the Lord makes rich,*
> *and he adds no sorrow with it.* (Proverbs 10:22)
>
> *Some freely give yet grow all the richer;*
> *others withhold what is due, and only suffer want.*
> (Proverbs 11:24)
>
> *The reward for humility and fear of the Lord*
> *is riches and honor and life.* (Proverbs 22:4)
>
> *By wisdom a house is built,*
> *and by understanding it is established;*

> *by knowledge the rooms are filled*
> *with all precious and pleasant riches.* (Proverbs 24:3–4)

King Solomon, moreover, stands as the great embodiment that wealth follows pious obedience:

> *I now do according to your word. Indeed I give you a wise and discerning mind; no one like you has been before you and no one like you shall arise after you. I give you also what you have not asked, both riches and honor all your life; no other king shall compare with you.* (1 Kings 3:12–13)

It is not different in the Sinai covenant of Israel that promises material blessing to those who keep Torah (Deuteronomy 28:1–15).

It was easy enough for the Puritans to take over this connection of *piety and wealth* under the rubric that piety would and did produce great accumulation. Before long, however, in the United States, the great accumulation of wealth became disconnected from genuine piety and made it an end so that making money and amassing wealth were readily taken as a vocation. Thus, the early claim of "providential blessing" was quickly converted into wealth for the sake of wealth. With that conversion of the old formula, wealth became a mark of virtue and, therefore, a powerful force in the political and public arena. We have fully embraced, in our society, the "Golden Rule": Those with the gold make the rules!

Consequently, government oversight and regulations are characteristically stacked in favor of wealth. The recent emergence of mega-billionaires like Elon Musk and Jeff Bezos has become a reiteration of the "robber barons" of a century ago, now without the restraints of antitrust legislation. To some great extent our political process is propelled by the force of wealth. Such wealth, evoked by limitless greed, is inimical to the neighbor love of the Torah and the gospel, for such wealth is inescapably and predictably dependent upon cheap labor. The extent to which church members arrive to worship with such a conviction of wealth as virtue is the extent to which the gospel's claims may cause discomfort or anxiety. It is the work of preaching, teaching, and interpretation to expose this contradiction to light and make it available for fresh decision-making.

2. The impetus toward territorial conquest has been intrinsic to Western Christianity since the earliest days of "Exploration and Discovery" when European adventurers set out for the New World. Propelled by a search for wealth, such explorers (and their patrons) were free to exploit the resources of the New World, including its human resources. The Church's early "Doctrine of Discovery" gave such European explorers the right to possess and plunder anything they could find. Thus, the Doctrine of Discovery led, over time, to wave after wave of colonialization, enslavement, and genocide.

The zeal for territorial conquest continued in the early colonies of the United States, as white settlers ruthlessly and relentlessly displaced the indigenous population with the claim of "Manifest Destiny." After settlement on the Atlantic Coast, the colonists pushed westward and "necessarily" eliminated the native populations. Finally, in 1828 the Doctrine of Discovery was read into US law by the Supreme Court so that the violent western push for the land had no restraint. With the settlement and conquest of the continent, the territorial imperative, under the leadership of Theodore Roosevelt and Woodrow Wilson, looked beyond the mainland to other "colonies and territories" under the imagined claim that the "natives" could not govern themselves.

I suppose that John F. Kennedy's spectacular "moon landing" on July 20, 1969 (in response to the Soviet Sputnik launch of October 4, 1957), was the ultimate symbol of territorial conquest. That elaborately staged event was readily taken to be a wondrous US triumph. This story of land possession without interruption or limit well served the US conviction of exceptionalism. As a result, Americans, including Christian Americans, could take this triumph as confirmation of entitlement and privilege among the peoples of the world. American

Christians could innocently sing of a global "mission" of the United States:

> *America, America!*
> *May God thy gold refine*
> *till all success be nobleness*
> *and every gain divine! . . .*
> *America, America!*
> *God shed his grace on thee,*
> *and crown thy good with brotherhood*
> *from sea to shining sea!*

These beloved words from "America the Beautiful" offer a coy combination of destiny, wealth, virtue, and land conquest as a gift from God. So now, American military power is established in hidden and neglected byways to assure Pax Americana worldwide. It helps that we can link this unending conquest of territory to the narrative of the book of Joshua, wherein the "chosen" people violently displace the indigenous population.

To the extent that this assumption of entitlement and privilege is shared among us, church worship is a jarring interruption. Such worship invites an alternative governance of *debts forgiven* and *bread shared.* This church worship calls into question our most fundamental societal assumptions of entitlement and privilege. It is enough to place us in crisis, or better, to bring to light the crisis we carry in our denial-driven bodies because we know better.

3. The creed of capitalism affirms that the natural world is a "storehouse of vendable wonders." The operative word is "vendable." Everything in the natural world can be transformed into a sellable product. Under the wise tutelage of Francis Bacon and John Locke, Christians were instructed in the fine art of private money-making that took the world as a viable commodity. See Cameron Whybrow,

The Bible, Baconianism, and Mastery over Nature: The Old Testament and Its Modern Misreading (1991). That passionate commercialization of the world gives no thought to "using up" or exhausting the material creation, for it is easily assumed that the supply is limitless. Thus, the spendthrift marketing of timber, water, oil, and whatever the land would produce has been unrestrained in service to the accumulation of private wealth. Exploiting natural resources follows from the sense of entitlement about the land (see above) and the limitless propulsion of wealth (see above). And now we have reached, in exhaustion, nearly to the end of "the Industrial Revolution" that saw the world as a commodity. The final exhaustion of the land of cotton plantations is a measure of the limits of commoditization wherein fruitful land has morphed into an endless patch of kudzu.

When we practitioners of land as commodity come to church, we are confronted with the claim that

> *The earth is the Lord's and all that is in it,*
> *the world and those who live in it.* (Psalm 24:1)

The lines ring in our ears! "Not ours!" Not mine to sell, not mine to exhaust. Not ours to use up! The current accent on environmentalism is a belated recognition of the claim that we, alongside the earth and its many diverse creatures, are yet creatures who stand in solidarity with other creatures in gladness before the creator of us all. This claim of *creator-creatures,* now given secular attestation in environmentalism, is the awareness that we are not users but caretakers. Church worship is an opportunity to sort out our identity with the earth and its other creatures. Such "sorting out" matters decisively because the difficult and urgent issue of creation as vulnerable and limited is not to be staged in grand theological utterance but through arguments about regulation, restraint, tax policy, and money-making at all costs. Church worship is an arena through which we may be repositioned in the world, not as masters but as co-creatures. We receive our life together from the creator and give it back to the creator in gratitude, generosity, and solidarity with other well-beloved creatures of God.

4. The repertoire of capitalism, McCarraher concludes, includes a "jeremiad tradition" fully ready for sharp indignation in moral judgments. In liberal churches, the jeremiad tends to concern social justice issues, and we make such fierce objections while we collude in the aforementioned ideology. Conversely, conservative, so-called evangelical churches specialize in jeremiads concerning moral failures concerning sexual and familial matters. But the jeremiads generally avoid the real questions to which McCarraher so well points. The jeremiads serve, as he says, to obscure the intractable persistence of the dilemma of being of two minds, *the mind of capitalism* and *the mind of the gospel*, that is, *the mind of God* and *the mind of Mammon.*

The church, at its most faithful, does not believe the dilemma is intractable. The church, in its worship, preaching, and teaching, has an opportunity to empower people (all of us!) to face the ambiguity we carry in our bodies. The point is not to place people in crisis but to bring visibility to our crisis. The crisis to be addressed is the elemental recognition that we are double-minded, and the double-mindedness is ultimately exhausting:

> *You cannot serve God and wealth.* (Matthew 6:24; Luke 16:13)

Or better, we cannot serve this God and mammon because they contradict each other. The church is the only place in town where that contradiction can be brought to light and speech, so fresh, practical, concrete decisions can be made. The point is not to scold anyone; that is an unproductive enterprise. Rather, it is to make available what we mostly manage to keep concealed from ourselves, namely, that it takes great energy to hide and deny the defining contradiction of our lives, the contradiction of God and capital.

So, imagine that the church and its pastors take the work of sorting out the ambiguity in practical ways as a proper inescapable task. We may together come to fresh awarenesses:

1. Wealth is no measure of being with God. Indeed, wealth cannot deliver on its manifold promises. Many folks have discovered through the Covid-19 pandemic that the real treasure to be valued is the value of sustainable relationships that can yield comfort, relief, and assurance. The work is to see that what we most value is not property or material accumulation; it is trustworthy relationships definitional for a viable life filled with well-being. Money can never and will never be a substitute for loyal relationships. Therefore, we in the church are committed to the practice of relationship that requires time, energy, and effort.

2. "Territorial conquest" may serve as a stand-in for every practice of wealth that requires anti-neighborly parsimonious violent action. The truth we always discover belatedly is that there is never enough material accumulation to make us safe or happy. There is always a need for more! Thus, in our zeal for "national security," for example, there is never enough, as yet, of armaments. There is always a need for expansion, newer security systems, and greater investment because restless uneasiness always belongs to such expansiveness.

I suppose the vision of disarmament in the prophetic oracle of Isaiah 2:2–4 is a welcome articulation of alternative:

> *They shall beat their swords into plowshares,*
> *and their spears into pruning hooks;*
> *nation shall not lift sword against nation,*
> *neither shall they learn war anymore.* (Isaiah 2:4)

Quite specifically, that same oracle in Micah 4:1–4 adds a line concerning an alternative life that is not included in the version of Isaiah:

> *But they shall all sit under their own vines and under their own*
> *fig trees,*
> *and none shall make them afraid;*
> *for the mouth of the Lord of hosts has spoken.* (Micah 4:4)

Disarmament of "spears into pruning hooks" is insufficient unless it is followed by a revamped economy that depends on changed appetites and desires. "Vine and fig tree" bespeak a sustainable quiet peasant life that satisfies modest desires and appetites. That is, the end of endless military aggression requires opting for an alternative social life that is satisfied with the resources and relationships of the neighborhood. That is the only viable alternative to ongoing conquest and conflict. It is a model of an alternative that the church can readily champion as a vote for a return to serious trustworthy relationality and in resistance to reliance upon greater and greater technological capacity.

3. As the church teaches and learns to revalue relationships that give meaning, identity, and body to our social existence, the world of vendable items becomes less and less compelling and persuasive. Such a practice invites us to shun the chance of being "rich in things and poor in soul" ("God of Grace and God of Glory," *Glory to God*, 307). What an alternative to being "rich in soul" and, to some extent, "poor in things!" Thus, we may indeed disengage from the world of commercialism and the norms of the market economy. There can hardly be a fuller embodiment of this alternative way of living than Jesus, who "had nowhere to lay his head" (Matthew 8:20). He lives from the generosity of the neighborhood, and his presence helped to evoke that generosity.

4. We know that it does no good to scold people. It also does no good to prattle on social justice in generic terms. In like manner, it does conservative, so-called evangelicals no good to rant about family values. We may be finished with all of that. We may better focus on the

wounds inflicted upon us and the wounds we inflict upon each other. We have enough sin and guilt to go around. But our preoccupation with sin—particularly other people's sin—is an effort in futility better that we consider how we may practice great interdependence and the risk of serious neighborly engagement.

We may imagine the church as a great forum of honesty that permits openness to our deep ambiguity, to walk into the ambiguity we carry in our bodies to make fresh decisions. The overriding issue, as McCarraher makes clear, is *God versus Mammon*. That large formulation of our dilemma invites us to consider the following:

- wealth vis-à-vis trustworthy relationships,
- territorial conquest vis-à-vis reliance on the neighborhood,
- vendable wonders vis-à-vis good social engagement, and
- jeremiads vis-à-vis honesty about wounds.

These are not grand theses. They are the realities of daily life where we act out our discipleship. Honesty in these matters might move us back toward our true selves and away from enslavement to market values. We gather to affirm and celebrate a life more fully congruent with our status as creatures loved and summoned by the creator to the wondrous tasks of creatureliness.

14

THE ADVENT OF AGENCY

I STUMBLED ONTO the book by Kelley Nikondeha, *The First Advent in Palestine: Reversals, Resistance, and the Ongoing Complexity of Hope* (2022), when asked by Broadleaf Books to write an endorsement for the book, which I did happily. I am quite moved by the book and commend it to you as a reader. The book is a reconsideration of the traditional Advent texts from Matthew and Luke read through the eyes of Palestinian suffering and oppression. Our use of the book may serve two purposes simultaneously: (a) to reflect in fresh ways on the Advent texts and (b) to offer a new awareness of the plight of Palestinians. The connection between Advent and the Palestinians is made by suggesting that the "first Advent," when the gospel narrative was first "performed," was in the midst of an oppressed people who the writers invited to revolutionary, transformative hope.

I will reflect only on Nikondeha's first chapter, "Silence and Suffering," through which she characterizes the sociopolitical scene in Palestine in the first century under Roman oppression. She appeals to the books of Maccabees and the public resistance that the Maccabees mounted against Roman oppression and exploitation. Specifically, Nikondeha notices the "laments" at the outset of 1 Maccabees, a powerful echo of Lamentations. Thus working backward, Roman oppression . . . the Maccabees . . . public lament . . . the book of Lamentations. In Lamentations, Israel grieved the destruction wrought by the Babylonians who had razed their beloved Jerusalem:

How lonely sits the city that was full of people!
How like a widow she has become, she that was great among the
nations!

She that was a princess among the provinces
has become a vassal.
She weeps bitterly in the night, with tears on her cheeks;
among all her lovers she has no one to comfort her;
all her friends have dealt treacherously with her,
they have become her enemies . . .
Is it nothing to you, all you who pass by?
Look and see if there is any sorrow like my sorrow,
which was brought upon me,
which the Lord inflicted on the day of his fierce anger.
(Lamentations 1:1–2, 12; see Psalm 137)

Nikondeha writes, referring to the initial Maccabees, Mattathias, father of five initiative-taking sons:

> *Maybe Mattathias reached for the book of Lamentations and recited the poems of grief handed down from the Jews before him. They had survived the Babylonian destruction of the first temple in 587 BCE and were acquainted with catastrophic loss. It was another time when the Jewish people were hard-pressed and left without the light of the Everlasting Flame.* (9)

In 1 Maccabees, we can identify laments that reflect in powerful ways the cadences of the older lamentations:

He [Antiochus] shed much blood,
and spoke with great arrogance.
Israel mourned deeply in every community,
rulers and elders groaned,
young women and young men became faint,
the beauty of the women faded.
Every bridegroom took up the lament;

she who sat in the bridal chamber was mourning.
Even the land trembled for its inhabitants,
and all the house of Jacob was clothed with shame.
(1 Maccabees 1:24–28)

For the citadel became an ambush against the sanctuary,
an evil adversary of Israel at all times.
On every side of the sanctuary they shed innocent blood;
they even defiled the sanctuary.
Because of them the residents of Jerusalem fled;
she became a dwelling of strangers;
she became strange to her offspring,
and her children forsook her.
Her sanctuary became desolate like a desert;
her feasts were turned to mourning,
her sabbaths to a reproach,
her honor into contempt.
Her dishonor now grew as great as her glory;
her exaltation was turned into mourning.
(1 Maccabees 1:36–40; see 2:7–13, 3:45, 50–53)

Now, I dwell on this two-step lament because, unlike Nikondeha, I suggest that lament is the appropriate posture for Christians at Advent. Note well that this is a very different accent from our usual emphasis on repentance—no doubt we have due cause for repentance. But before we get to that, Lamentations is a vigorous out-loud recognition of our loss of an old world we treasured that has departed. Thus, in Lamentations, the loss concerned the ancient, beloved city of Jerusalem with its king and temple, all terminated by the Babylonians. For the Maccabees in the second century BCE, it was obvious enough that the predatory Roman Empire only imitated the exploitation of Babylon so that a new inventory of laments was properly sounded.

I propose that the theme and out-loud practice of lament is a proper way to engage in the Advent season. The work of Christians might well be a deep, shared articulation of loss among us. We may indeed grieve loss:

- Concerning *the demise of the old established church* of the Eisenhower years, when church participation was normal and taken for granted. All that is gone now! The quest now is for a new faithful form of church that is not dependent upon buildings, programs, and staff but is rather occupied with missional witness and sacramental practice of song and prayer. That loss is due cause for lament.
- Concerning *the disappearance of the old white male world of control and privilege* (with its tacit assumption of heterosexuality). That world was for some a wondrous life of well-being and certainty in which people of color and all sorts of others (who were "lesser") lived in conformist silence and subordination. Some neo-evangelicals still want to ensure that the old world is recoverable and kept intact. But it is gone! While some are glad about that, a large body of our society must grieve in acknowledgment of that loss beyond recovery so that it may be knowingly relinquished.
- Concerning *the singular dominance of the United States* when "America" was "manifestly" God's chosen people and could do whatever it wanted in the world. That limitless capacity is now harshly checked by the rise of China as a world power, and all the brave nationalist talk will not reverse that new historical reality. We may prattle that we may "Make America Great Again," but we must come to terms with a new world, not of our making.

There is so much to lament when we think of the "good old days" that were "good" only for some among us. There is so much among us that is to be wept . . . all that loss! Advent is preparation for a "newness coming" that requires relinquishing what is old and gone, even if the old has a deep and insistent grip upon us. The act of lament is a public form of truth-telling in spite of our continuing wish for otherwise. It is an act that crowds in upon our shared propensity for denial. There is no one, moreover, to be truthful about our common loss except the church and the synagogue and their shared legacy of honest truth-telling about loss. That work is urgent and must be addressed.

That voicing of loss in Lamentations is almost unrelieved. Indeed the book ends with an unanswered question about rejection (5:22). There is, nonetheless, a moment of relief in Lamentations that is often noticed:

> *The steadfast love of the Lord never ceases,*
> *his mercies never come to an end;*
> *they are new every morning;*
> *great is your faithfulness.* (3:22–23)

Right in the middle of the loss, Israel, in its lament, commits a bold act of remembering, returns to the old tradition, and finds their compelling witness to the fidelity of God. This fidelity is not interrupted by present calamity. These two verses speak the counter themes that are often reiterated in Israel's praise:

- *steadfast love* . . . tenacious fidelity!
- *mercy* . . . voiced in the plural!
- *faithfulness* . . . utter reliability!

For an instant amid its lament, Israel can pause to remember and affirm.

In the same way it is possible in the church, amid lament over our loss of the *traditional church*, *traditional culture*, and *dominant nationalism*, to give voice to assurances about God's fidelity that persists in and through our deepest losses, and is not disrupted by those losses. Thus, we have loss to lament, but then we come to affirmation. The church can celebrate that affirmation in the face of lament, but that affirmation leads to neither resignation nor complacency. Rather, it leads to *agency*, to the readiness and capacity to act in constructive, imaginative ways in defiance toward newness. This process evokes an eagerness to celebrate and perform newness amid the shambles of loss in Israel. In ancient Israel that move from lament through fidelity to agency is performed, for example, by Nehemiah, an exiled Jew who served in the Persian court. Nehemiah knew about loss, lament, and grief:

> *When I heard these words [concerning the devastation of Jerusalem], I sat down and wept, and mourned for days, fasting and praying before the God of heaven. I said, "O Lord God of heaven, the great and awesome God who keeps covenant and steadfast love with those who love him and keep his commandments; let your ear be attentive and your eyes open to hear the prayer of your servant that I now pray before you day and night for your servants, the people of Israel . . . Lord, let your ear be attentive to the prayer of your servant, and to the prayer of your servants who delight in revering your name. Give success to your servant today, and grant him mercy in the sight of this man!" [that is, the Persian king]* (Nehemiah 1:4–11)

Nehemiah's grief, however, did not lead him to passivity. Rather, when he had the chance, a chance created by his grief noticed by the Persian king, he explained his grief to the king:

> *Why should not my face be sad, when the city, the place of my ancestors' graves, lies waste, and its gates have been destroyed by fire?* (2:3)

This acknowledgment of grief and devastation is followed immediately by a request to the king that he be dispatched by royal favor and with royal resources back to the ruined city of Jerusalem:

> *If it pleases the king, and if your servant has found favor with you, I ask that you send me to Judah, the city of my ancestors' graves, so that I may rebuild it.* (2:5)

The remainder of the book follows the course of Nehemiah's restorative actions.

The case is not different for Ezra, the scribe who served alongside Nehemiah. Ezra is capable of deep, honest lament:

> *O Lord, God of Israel, you are just, but we have escaped as a remnant, as is now the case. Here we are before you in our guilt, though no one can face you because of this.* (Ezra 9:15)

> *Here we are, slaves to this day—slaves in the land that you gave to our ancestors to enjoy its fruit and its good gifts. Its rich yield goes to the kings whom you have set over us because of our sins; they have power also over our bodies and over our livestock at their pleasure, and we are in great distress.* (Nehemiah 9:36–37)

Ezra's grief-cum-guilt did not lead to his passivity, but to constructive action. Above all, in Nehemiah 8, Ezra leads the community in the fresh articulation of faith by reintroducing Torah, resulting in a Torah-based community that could readily distinguish itself knowingly from the world around.

Thus, the reading of Nikondeha has led me to think about the sequence of:

grief voiced,
hope reiterated, and
agency embraced.

I suggest this may be a workable way to enter the Advent season and its texts. Nikondeha considers in some detail the traditional Advent texts that come as reassurance and summons to those who have engaged in the honesty of grief.

It is not difficult to imagine this practice of Advent if the church has the courage and will to resist the commercial pressure of Christmas coming too soon. The church will be profoundly at odds with our commercial context at every step in this process.

- instead of denial . . . *grief,*
- instead of self-indulgent complacency . . . *hope,*
- instead of resignation . . . *agency!*

The bet is that in doing so the church will offer honesty for which many people yearn, even as they may dread facing it. Thus, our task might be:

- The *honest articulation of loss* that is all around us. Conservatives and evangelicals are not the only ones who have a long, deep attachment to the way the world has been in former time. But imagine a congregation, altogether, actually naming the loss of current forms of church, culture, and national preeminence. This catalog of losses allows for us to include in the process more intimate, personal, and hidden losses as well.
- The *bold unrestrained articulation of God's fidelity*. This will permit and require an affirmation that is more frontal and scandalous than a generic hope for love all around us. The testimony is to the God who has the whole created world held in safe hands and who, in Israel's memory, has performed mighty deeds of

transformation. In Christian cadence, these transformative deeds come to the fullest form in the narrative of Jesus. There can be nothing anemic in this affirmation.

- The *summons that the gospel issues* is that those to whom God is available in hope are empowered to have agency, to be about the good work of restoration and rehabilitation. In the case of Ezra and Nehemiah that work was the restoration of Judaism. In the case of the Maccabees the work was to resist Rome, a resistance that led to the restoration of the Jerusalem temple (and the festival Hanukkah).

In our own time and place those who grieve honestly and hope well are summoned and empowered to like work of restoration and rehabilitation.

- The *rehabilitation and restoration of the church* will require a re-engagement with the most elemental claims of the gospel, and thus to missional engagement for the work of God's neighborly emancipation and restoration.
- The *rehabilitation and restoration of our culture* will require the creation of a neighborly multi-cultural fabric that takes each neighbor seriously and offers an infrastructure to secure the dignity, safety, and well-being of each neighbor, no matter how vulnerable they may be.
- The *restoration and rehabilitation of our national state* includes fostering democratic practices that protect the public voice of every potential voter and the refusal of the anti-democratic efforts to reduce the influence of the many for the sake of control by the few.

Nikondeha reads the Advent texts in the context of the original population of the left-behind and the vulnerable who are the antecedents of, among others, current Palestinians. She shows, moreover, that the Advent texts are the launching pad for the narrative summons to follow in the gospel accounts that constitute a call to costly discipleship. Thus, in the gospel of Matthew it takes only until chapter 4 for the summons to be issued:

> *As he walked by the Sea of Galilee, he saw two brothers, Simon, who is called Peter, and Andrew his brother, casting a net into the sea—for they were fishermen. And he said to them, "*Follow *me, and I will make you fish for people." Immediately they left their nets and followed him. As he went from there, he saw two brothers, James son of Zebedee and his brother John, in the boat with their father Zebedee, mending their nets, and he called them. Immediately they left the boat and their father, and* followed *him.* (Matthew 4:18–22)

In the Gospel of Luke, the same account is in chapter 5:

> *For he and all who were with him were amazed at the catch of fish they had taken; and so also were James and John, sons of Zebedee, who were partners with Simon. Then Jesus said to Simon, "Do not be afraid; from now on you will be catching people." When they had brought their boats to shore, they left everything and* followed *him.* (Luke 5:9–11)

The summons comes more readily in the Gospel of Mark:

> *As Jesus passed along the Sea of Galilee, he saw Simon and his brother Andrew casting a net into the sea—for they were fishermen. And Jesus said to them, "*Follow *me, and I will make you fish for people." And immediately they left their nets and followed him. As he went a little further, he saw James son of Zebedee and his brother John, who were in their boat mending the nets. Immediately he called them; and they*

> *left their father Zebedee in the boat with the hired men, and* followed *him.* (Mark 1:16–20)

The matter is early and somewhat different in the Gospel of John:

> *The next day John again was standing with two of his disciples, and as he watched Jesus walk by, he exclaimed, "Look, here is the Lamb of God!" The two disciples heard him say this, and they* followed *Jesus.* (John 1:35–37)

The Advent texts are not freestanding; they are openers for what is to follow. They are transcripts of grief and hope that issue in agency.

Jesus of course knows Israel's lament tradition well. He reiterates the tradition of grief concerning the failure and fragility of Jerusalem, the citadel of power that is now wholly in jeopardy.

> *Jerusalem, Jerusalem, the city that kills the prophets and stones those who are sent to it! How often have I desired to gather your children together as a hen gathers her brood under her wings, and you were not willing!* (Luke 13:34)

> *As he came near and saw the city, he wept over it, saying, "If you, even you, had only recognized on this day the things that make for peace! But now they are hidden from your eyes. Indeed, the days will come upon you, when your enemies will set up ramparts around you and surround you, and hem you in on every side. They will crush you to the ground, you and your children within you, and they will not leave within you one stone upon another; because you did not recognize the time of your visitation from God."* (Luke 19:41–44)

Advent is our "time of the visitation from God!" Advent is a time to recognize that visitation and to sign on for the new regime that is "at hand." It may indeed be that this sequence of *grief/hope/agency* will enable the church to resist the commercial reductionism of our culture and to engage in the good work of the new world. Nikondeha ends her rich and suggestive book in this way:

> *Each reversal in the advent narrative is a seed tossed into the soil, placed for hope to take root. Zechariah, Elizabeth, Mary, Joseph, and the shepherds are the grassroots practitioners showing us the hope that erodes empires. Among the tools we are given by the first advent in Palestine are hospitality, solidarity, and nonviolence—ready for the hopeful to use as we subvert the empires God will one day bring to an end.*
>
> *As the magi don't just see the star from the East and marvel at it, we learn from them to act in hope and follow the star that guides us. We travel in the light of that star, in and through the trajectory of the advent story toward—always—resurrection!* (86–87)

15

ON GERRYMANDERING TEXTS

WE ALL KNOW about gerrymandered congressional districts. Whenever they can, Republicans and Democrats skew district lines, misrepresent social reality, and grasp for disproportionate power and influence. In the wake of that reality of which we are all aware, I want to consider here the "gerrymandering of biblical texts," my phrase for biblical texts read aloud in the congregation that boldly and openly skip over verses to accent other verses the pastor believes the church most needs to hear. This is a common practice in non-lectionary congregations, but it is also a practice common enough in the lectionary itself. Case in point: I was recently at worship on "All Saints Sunday." The chosen non-lectionary reading for the day was Revelation 22:12–21, a quite appropriate text for the Sunday with its articulation of the ultimate promise of the gospel. In our hearing, however, we were allowed only verses 12–14, 16–17, and 20–21, a sure sign of gerrymandering.

The parts of the text we were permitted to hear were glorious and wondrous in their offer. The God who speaks and promises to come is the Alpha and the Omega (vv. 12–13). Then in verses 16–17 it is Jesus who speaks. He issues a threefold "Come," an invitation to "the water of the tree of life." Finally, "the one who testifies" promises to come soon with a blessing of grace for "all the saints" (vv. 20–21). The sum of these chosen verses is a generous welcome to all for the riches and well-being of life to come presided over by the generosity of God. The invitation is an offer to "everyone," except that we may notice that even in verse 12, which was read, the God who comes soon will "repay according to everyone's work." Apart from the verses skipped over, that is such a minor note that we scarcely notice it.

When I saw printed in the bulletin for Sunday that the text was "gerrymandered," I was curious about the parts held back in silence. Of course I was not terribly surprised by what I found. In verse 15 (skipped over!), there is a sharp contrast between the "blessed" who are given access to "the tree of life" and the others who are characterized as "dogs, sorcerers, fornicators, murderers, and idolaters," all of those who live fake lives.

> *Outside are the dogs and sorcerers and fornicators and murderers and idolaters, and everyone who loves and practices falsehood.* (v. 15)

This negative catalog fairly closely shadows the Ten Commandments. I could readily see why a pastor would not want to read these lines aloud in the church. Not only are the lines quite polemical, but they just might encourage self-righteousness among the "blessed." The other verses also skipped over are verses 18–19:

> *I warn everyone who hears the words of the prophecy of this book: If anyone adds to them, God will add to that person the plagues described in this book; if anyone takes away from the words of the book of this prophecy, God will take away that person's share in the tree of life and in the holy city, which are described in this book.* (vv. 18–19)

These verses warn anyone who tampers with Revelation, "the prophecy of this book." The warning is twofold: don't add to it or take away from it. Those who "add" to it will get the plague on them; those who "take away" from it will have taken away from them a share of "the tree of life in the holy city." The penalties are severe: Don't do it! Let the text stand. There may be some wee irony in that the pastors who left out these verses are among those who "take away" from the text. Well, of course, no one wants to read aloud such severe stuff, and besides that, there is not a single person in the congregation who has an iota of interest in editing the book of Revelation!

As is almost always the case, this gerrymandering of the text is to leave out the hard parts so that we are left with an all-welcoming, all-embracing offer of the goodness of God without any exceptions or any noticeable ground for exclusion. This is indeed free grace! Even if it might risk the extreme of "cheap grace."

I understand that no pastor wants to read the hard stuff aloud; neither do I. I get it that no congregation wants to hear the hard stuff; neither do I as a congregant. And so we gerrymander, innocently attentive, with regularity. And we are left with a cushy gospel of love, sweet love. No exclusions in the end!

If ever such gerrymandering needs to be justified, we rightly say that our norm is not "scripture." Our norm is the "gospel." And if parts of scripture do not serve the gospel they can be readily silenced. And so we often make that judgment. But such subjective judgments might leave us uneasy, especially if we were to ask what the text is really about. Thus, I want to suggest that a welcome alternative to gerrymandering the text is *the good hard work of teaching*. Therefore, the interpreter might take the trouble to start with the text and show the congregation what is at stake in the text.

We know that Revelation is written by and for the church when it was under heavy assault by the Roman Empire. In the face of pressure to trust in and live out the gospel, members of the early church were subject to harsh treatment from the empire. As a result, many Christians readily compromised with the demands and expectations of the empire, not blinking at compromising the gospel. Revelation was written to urge Christians under threat not to compromise their faith, but to have the courage and tenacity essential to faith. If we begin with this awareness, then the initial warning of verse 12 (over which we have skipped) makes sense. "Everyone's work" concerns obedience to the gospel . . . or not. And thus it turns out that the catalog of condemnations in verse 15 concerns the "falsehood" of selling out to Rome.

The piling up of condemnatory terms in verse 15 is not to be taken with specificity but is a cluster of terms concerning those who have compromised their faith. It follows that those who "add" to or "take away" in verses 18–19 are those who want to gerrymander the faith concerning the hard either/or that the church faces vis-à-vis Rome. Thus, the entire text is a contrast between those who have kept faith and those who find faith too demanding and so compromise. This is a very different point from the generous proclamation that all (on All Saints Sunday!) are offered an easy welcome, regardless of "everyone's work."

The point of taking the text seriously is surely not to scold people. Rather, it is to help people in the church understand the demanding circumstance of Christians in the ancient world of Rome, and then to articulate the demanding circumstance of the church in our current social context. Of course our current demanding circumstance is not so sharp and clear—all the more difficult to notice it! But in truth we current Christians in US society are indeed placed in a demanding circumstance:

- We are invited to the easy life of consumerism that lets us be self-preoccupied.
- We are tempted to privatized, individualized capitalism, a force that shows up concretely and unmistakably in our current unjust health care system.
- We are beset by a *pax Americana* in which, like ancient Rome, we can imagine that our imperial military reach is an unmitigated good.
- We are confronted by a long-standing unyielding policy and practice of racism (that in my neighborhood concerns Native Americans as much as it involves Blacks).
- We are tempted to economic fear, so that even in the congregation's relative affluence, we are sobered by pressures unrelated to our actual financial circumstance.

All these issues—to which others may easily be added—are powerful reasons to compromise the gospel and impede the congregation's missional work.

The text is an invitation, negatively, to *resist and refuse such compromises.* It is an invitation, positively, to *remain faithful to the gospel's claims,* even against the stress of dominant opinion. The text is a promise to the "blessed" who will let the refrain of "the prophecy of this book" ring in our ears, a ringing that reminds us of our baptismal vocational identity. The other point I want to accent is that it is better and more responsible to do our work of interpretation that moves from an ancient context demanding faith to our contemporary context demanding faith than to gerrymander. It is better, because it more clearly serves our sense of calling to be who we are "in Christ."

Gerrymandering the text is generally to avoid the hard work of interpretation and offer a gospel that comes without demand. The church is ill-served by such a procedure, because gerrymandering is a practice of leaving out some of what must be said and what must be heard in the church.

- Gerrymandering is not unlike an honest conversation between love partners when we do not say what hurts because it is easier not to say that. Thus "I forgot."
- Gerrymandering is not unlike being honest with a therapist but finding it too hard to say something out loud, present in favorable light an acceptable self, and say, "Oh, I forgot."

Gerrymandering is a willful forgetting of what can be said and often must be said in the church. The church is to receive "the whole counsel of God," not simply the liturgist's preferences or the congregation itself (Acts 20:27).

In the United States, we are in for tough days in the church. We might better prepare the church for those hard days to come by articulating the gospel in its fully generous and demanding scope. The church is ill-served by scripture reading that lets us imagine that the Holy One is indifferent to our choices and the risks we run or refuse to run. Sometimes, of course, the church is to be nourished with the milk of the gospel that is for babies (1 Peter 2:2). But sometimes what is required is a full diet of the truth of the gospel that is harder to swallow than sweet milk. I suspect that in many cases the church is more ready to receive the fullness of the gospel than we preachers are wont to offer. The "grace" on offer in the last verse of the Bible is not cheap grace. It is for "all the saints," those who have had a chance to answer to the gospel's call that is sometimes issued in hard circumstances. Let the church have an ear to "listen to what the Spirit is saying to the church," every syllable of it (Revelation 2:7). It is likely the case that a church that often gerrymanders the text will have among its company many who are "lukewarm" (Revelation 3:16).

16

ELECT FROM EVERY NATION YET ONE O'ER ALL THE EARTH*

I HAVE BEEN thinking about "being chosen" since my high school days. In my high school (Blackburn, Missouri) of twenty-seven kids, there were eleven boys. But since Leslie Cook had a bad heart, there were ten of us to play basketball. Almost every day we "chose" sides for basketball scrimmage. The choosing always went the same way. First, Donald Buck, Buddy Borchers, and my brother Ed were chosen. They were by all odds the best players. I was among those in the middle range who were chosen next. At the end of the process were three kids who were never chosen, but simply "divvied up" by the choosers. As I recall, these

---

* My title phrase is from the hymn "The Church's One Foundation," *Glory to God*, 321. The complete second stanza goes like this:

> *Elect from every nation, yet one o'er all the earth,*
> *her charter of salvation;*
> *one Lord, one faith, one birth.*
> *One holy name she blesses, partakes one holy food,*
> *and to one hope she presses, with every grace endued.*

The verse offers a summary of the claims and bases of chosenness:

- chosenness as verification of salvation
- one Lord and one faith as attested in the two great creeds of the church
- one birth, that is, baptism
- only the name of Christ in whom we are chosen
- the holy food of Eucharist
- hope that is grace-propelled but that entails obedience

three boys were allowed to run up and down the court, but never were passed the ball. They continued to be the unchosen!

This all came to mind when I saw a church street sign near us at "Fellowship Church": "God has Chosen You to be His." The sign is, of course, unembarrassed about its masculine pronoun. Beyond that, the statement is so generic as to be meaningless, even if it expresses a truth about the God of the gospel. In any case, the sign made me think about being chosen (on which see my little book, *Chosen: Reading the Bible amid the Israeli-Palestinian Conflict*, 2015).

The Old Testament revolves around the notion of Israel as God's chosen people. The Sinai tradition articulates the claim of chosenness with a strong "if" of conditionality:

> *Now therefore, if you obey my voice and keep my covenant,*
> *you shall be my treasured possession out of all the peoples.*
> *Indeed, the whole earth is mine, but you shall be for me a*
> *priestly kingdom and a holy nation.* (Exodus 19:5–6)

In the tradition of Deuteronomy, however, the "if" of Torah conditionality is subdued because God's choosing of Israel is located in YHWH's own inclination that requires no explanation or justification:

> *For you are a people holy to the Lord your God; the Lord*
> *your God has chosen you out of all the peoples on the earth*
> *to be his people, his treasured possession. It was not because*
> *you were more numerous than any other people that the Lord*
> *set his heart on you and chose you—for you were the fewest*
> *of all peoples. It was because the Lord loved you and kept*
> *the oath that he swore to your ancestors, that the Lord has*
> *brought you out with a mighty hand, and redeemed you from*
> *the house of slavery, from the hand of Pharaoh king of Egypt.*
> (Deuteronomy 7:6–8)

> *Although heaven and the heaven of heavens belongs to the Lord your God, the earth with all that is in it, yet the Lord set his heart in love on your ancestors alone and chose you, their descendants after them, out of all the peoples, as it is today.* (10:14–15)

The same ambiguity pertains concerning God's choosing of David and his dynasty. In Psalm 132, God's promise to the dynasty is governed by an "if":

> *The Lord swore to David a sure oath from which he will not*
> *turn back:*
> *"One of the sons of your body I will set on your throne.*
> *If your sons keep my covenant and my decrees that I shall teach*
> *them,*
> *their sons also, forevermore, shall sit on your throne."*
> (Psalm 132: 11–12)

But in Psalm 89, the "if" of conditionality has disappeared in a sure promise:

> *You said, "I have made a covenant with my chosen one,*
> *I have sworn to my servant David:*
> *'I will establish your descendants forever,*
> *and build your throne for all generations.'"* . . .
> *Forever I will keep my steadfast love for him,*
> *and my covenant with him will stand firm.*
> *I will establish his line forever,*
> *and his throne as long as the heavens endure.*
> *If his children forsake my law and do not walk according to my*
> *ordinances,*
> *if they violate my statutes and do not keep my commandments,*

> *then I will punish their transgression with the rod and their*
> *iniquity with scourges;*
> *but I will not remove from him my steadfast love,*
> *or be false to my faithfulness.*
> *I will not violate my covenant,*
> *or alter the word that went forth from my lips.*
> *Once and for all I have sworn by my holiness;*
> *I will not lie to David.*
> *His line shall continue forever,*
> *and his throne endure before me like the sun.*
> *It shall be established forever like the moon,*
> *an enduring witness in the skies.* (Psalm 89:3–4, 28–37)

To be sure, verses 30 to 31 include an "if" of obedience, but that "if" is now fully and finally subordinated to the ringing claim of "forever" (vv. 28, 29, 36, 37). In this regard Psalm 89 echoes the narrative affirmation of 2 Samuel 7:

> *When he commits iniquity, I will punish him with a rod such as mortals use, with blows inflicted by human beings. But I will not take my steadfast love from him, as I took it from Saul, whom I put away from before you. Your house and your kingdom shall be made sure forever before me; your throne shall be established forever.* (vv. 14–16)

Punishment and/or judgment are quite penultimate in their relationship. What counts is the unqualified commitment of YHWH to the dynasty as to the people.

This is enough to see that the notion of "chosen" was, from the outset, problematic in Israel. On the one hand, it is conditioned by obedience; on the other hand, it is fully unconditional. Its problematic character becomes more evident in the prophetic tradition. On the one hand, the prophets could entertain the thought that God's harshness toward disobedient Israel could be so severe as to signify the ending of Israel as chosen. On the other hand and quickly, the prophets readily affirmed God's commitment to Israel that would, in the rhetoric of prophetic promise, "make all things new" for Israel, according to God's durable promises. The tradition does not need to resolve this problematic, but keeps available different accents appropriate to varying circumstances in the life of Israel.

I think we might articulate the deep problematic of chosenness in this way: Chosenness is *a powerful tool of community formation and maintenance* among those who have few claims and few resources, and who are vulnerable amid the give and take of public life. Chosenness is a way to gather identity and mobilize purpose for the "mixed crowd" that has no sense of people-hood (see Exodus 12:37). Conversely, chosenness becomes *a narcotic and an alibi* when the community becomes strong and powerful, so that its claim of chosenness becomes an excuse for destructive, exploitative action and a justification for willful anti-neighborly conduct. Thus, "election" works well for the weak and vulnerable, but is misleading and distorting for the strong and powerful. Its misuse is evident in the exploitative power of the church throughout its history, in the overstatement of White American exceptionalism, and even in the contemporary state of Israel.

The early church appropriated the claim of chosenness from Israel, and did so in a way that smacked of supersessionism. Now it could claim that the community of Christ—the church—was the chosen community, a community formed of "nobodies" who were summoned and empowered by the gospel for witness and obedience. Thus, Paul could celebrate this new community constituted by the foolish, the weak, the low and despised:

> *But God chose what is foolish in the world to shame the wise; God chose what is weak in the world to shame the strong; God chose what is low and despised in the world, things that are not, to reduce to nothing things that are.* (1 Corinthians 1:27–28)

Such a community is a good match for the God whose foolishness is wise and whose weakness is strong:

> *For God's foolishness is wiser than human wisdom, and God's weakness is stronger than human strength.* (1 Corinthians 1:25)

The same affirmation is made in the Epistle of Peter in grand, sweeping language reminiscent of the rhetoric of Sinai:

> *But you are a chosen race, a royal priesthood, a holy nation,*
> *God's own people, in order that you may proclaim the mighty acts of him who called you out of darkness into his marvelous light.*
> *Once you were not a people,*
> *but now you are God's people;*
> *once you had not received mercy,*
> *but now you have received mercy.* (1 Peter 2:9–10)

The *"not a people"* who have become *the people of God* matches the Christ who is the stone the builders have rejected that has become the head of the corner (v. 7).

In both the traditions of Paul and Peter the church as chosen is constituted by those who have neither power nor credentials in the world. And so the status of "chosenness" serves well in order to form the chosen of a faithful church. But of course as the church historically came to power, the matter of "church as chosen" became exceedingly vexatious. Cases in point run from the *medieval crusades* to the modern world of *violent usurpatious Western colonialism* wherein the cross went along with the flag, down to present-day habits of *sexual predation* among church leaders. All of these are instances of "chosenness" made into an excuse for conduct and policy that exhibit greed and covetousness that are inimical to the God who chooses.

It may be that the "Fellowship Church," in its sign, intends to appeal to the un-chosen in our community without significant social identity or resources. It is mind-boggling to imagine the three boys always un-chosen for basketball in my high school being the first chosen, or perhaps even made captains who would choose the teams. None of that occurred to us back then.

So perhaps we are left with this question: *Who are the chosen among us?* Jews will continue to claim their chosen status. And the Church will continue to sing of itself as "elect from every nation." After these traditional claims are reiterated and regarded by many as decisive and definitional, we may still ask afresh: Who are the chosen among us? Who are those chosen as the special object of God's love and compassion, mercy, and justice? Who are the chosen as the preferred recipients of our common social resources? When we ask at the same time about both *the object of God's love* and *recipients of our common social resources*, we may be pushed toward, in the parsing of Liberation Theology, "God's preferential option for the poor." Given what we know of the Torah, the prophets, and the witness of Christ, we can readily conclude that the chosen are not those with power and resources, but precisely those without power or resources.

In the Torah and the prophetic tradition, the triad of such people are "widows, orphans, and immigrants," those without social standing or property, and without advocacy in a patriarchal society. To these three are sometimes added a fourth, "the poor," because in such a patriarchal society, "widows, orphans, and immigrants" are likely to be poor and without resources or social power. In the narrative of Jesus, those who are recipients of his special, transformative attention are the blind, the lame, the lepers, the deaf, the dead, and the poor (see Luke 7:22). Jesus went about "choosing" such folk to receive his restorative mercy and compassion.

So now we may conclude, in the wake of the Torah, the prophetic tradition, and the witness of Jesus, that the chosen are all those "left behind" by the calculus of the market, all those who do not "qualify" as insiders to the capitalist system who are left behind in health care, housing, and education. That includes many people of color, poor people, children, old people, and disabled people. It is for good reason that when Jesus responded to the question of John the Baptist with his catalog of the chosen, he added:

> *And blessed is anyone who takes no offense at me.*
> (Luke 7:23)

The validation of such folk is indeed an offense. It is an offense to imagine such folk as recipients of God's special love. It is an even greater offense to think that such folk should and must receive the community's resources for their well-being. But this conclusion seems unavoidable, given the tradition. It is the business and the responsibility of the communities of this tradition, synagogue and church, to be advocates in the public domain for these "chosen." It may be what "Fellowship Church" intends. It certainly never occurred to us back in high school. It never occurred to us, because the church has not been a good teacher of this claim and the problematic of chosenness. But now we are without excuse. We can no longer exercise the violent exploitation of the status of chosenness wherein we have dared to imagine that those with power and wealth could be "the chosen." The tradition tells us otherwise, in quite unambiguous terms!

Part III

THE EMANCIPATION OF THE NEIGHBORHOOD

17

THE PATHETIC IMAGINATION

SINCE THE PUBLICATION of my book, *The Prophetic Imagination*, in 1978, I have returned to its theme many times. I have concluded that "prophetic imagination" consists of the capacity to host a world other than the one in front of us. Thus, the ancient prophets in Israel lived in a world propelled by money, power, wisdom, fear, and violence. But the world to which they bore witness was very different. That world, given mostly in poetic imagery, is one where God governs with a will for justice and compassion. In that imagined world they bore witness, God has a ready, willing capacity to create joyous viable conditions for life. In that world, moreover, the greedy toxic ways of our present world stand under prompt judgment. The world they host is very different from the one in front of Israel that was managed mostly to eliminate God as a serious player and a real character.

The other day I was talking, yet again, about "prophetic imagination." In a slip of the tongue I inadvertently said, "pathetic imagination." That slip has led me to reflect on how "pathetic imagination" is very different from "prophetic imagination." Pathetic imagination is incapable of hosting an alternative world and remains quite satisfied to have its sphere of possibility circumscribed to the small world in front of us. Thus, in the confines of pathetic imagination, the claims of prophetic imagination are outrageous and incredible.

As I began to think about pathetic imagination and its severe limitations, I thought of a clear example in the Old Testament. In 2 Kings 6:8–23 the unnamed king of Syria, the perennial enemy of ancient Israel, is yet again at war with Israel. The king of Syria is convinced that Elisha, the prophet, is a spy in the service of Israel's unnamed king. As a result, the Syrian king dispatches a mighty military host to surround Elisha's house to seize him.

In the narrative Elisha's aide looks out of the window and see the Syrian soldiers and horses. That is all he can see, and he is very frightened:

> *Alas, master! What shall we do?* (2 Kings 6:16)

The aide can see that he and Elisha are helpless, outnumbered and without resources, and therefore vulnerable to this military company. It turns out that the frightened response of the aide to what he saw out of the window is a compelling example of pathetic imagination. He can see only what is in front of him, enough to frighten him.

His faulty vision and his fear are countered by Elisha who, in an unflappable way, offers prophetic imagination. That is, his capacity to see otherwise. He reassures his aide:

> *Do not be afraid, for there are more with us than there are with them.* (v. 17)

The aide thinks that Elisha cannot count very well, or he is utilizing some "new math." Through his prayer Elisha makes it possible for his aide to see what he now sees that had remained invisible to him:

> *So the Lord opened the eyes of the servant, and he saw; the mountain was full of horses and chariots of fire all around Elisha.* (v. 17)

It turns out that according to this act of prophetic imagination the world was very different from the one permitted by the pathetic imagination of the aide.

We have no way of knowing what the reality of Elisha's "revealment" was, but it was in any case enough to subdue the Syrian force and make it helpless. Elisha led the helpless Syrians to Samaria and presented them to the Israelite king. Prophetic imagination goes even further, because Elisha resists the intention of the Israelite king to kill the Syrians. Instead, Elisha hosts a great feast and sends them home. In the narrative the prophet contradicts the pathetic imagination of both his aide and his king. The outcome is a long period of peace between Israel and Syria. We of course notice that the narrative does not "explain" anything. It leaves the narrative for us to ponder, and to consider how it might be that alternative imagination yields alternative historical reality and alternative historical outcomes. We may take the aide and the Israelite king to be representatives of pathetic imagination that fails, in fear and in dullness to reckon with a world in which the living God is an effective player.

In the New Testament we may trace, especially in the Gospel of Matthew, the pathetic imagination of the disciples of Jesus who are said four times to be people of "little faith" (*oligopistoi*).

Jesus chides his disciples for being anxious about food and clothing, when they are able to observe the bounty of God's creation in even more transient things.

> *But if God so clothes the grass of the field, which is alive today and tomorrow is thrown into the oven, will he not much more clothe you—you of little faith.* (Matthew 6:30; see Luke 12:28)

Their anxiety is an outcome of "little faith," that is, pathetic imagination that cannot host a world of God's abundance when they are fixed on their own needs and deficiencies. The alternative to such anxiety is to be focused instead on the reception of God's rule of righteousness.

In another episode, the disciples are out on the sea during a great storm. They are very frightened and say, "We are perishing" (Matthew 8:25). Jesus reprimands his disciples for their little faith:

Why are you afraid, you of little faith? (Matthew 8:26)

If we understand the storm as an instance of the threat of chaos, faith might have reassured the disciples that God the creator has got the whole world in his hands, including chaos. After his reprimand, Jesus stills the chaotic waters, thus performing and exhibiting the ordering work of the creator. It is no wonder that the disciples are amazed to see that even the chaotic waters and wind obey "this man," the creator God among them. Their fear had overridden whatever faith they may have had in the creator God.

In a third text the narrative features only Peter who faces the chaotic waters and a strong wind (Matthew 14:28–33). Again, the force of the storm frightens Peter and causes him to panic. Again, Jesus rebukes him for his little faith because he doubts the capacity of Jesus to master the wind and water. But Jesus rescues him and stills the storm. He is recognized as the "Son of God." Those in the boat could readily recognize that Jesus had overridden the fear of Peter by acting as the creator who could order the wind. It is no wonder that they worshiped him!

In a fourth episode, the disciples are fearful because they have no bread (Matthew 16:5–12). It turns out that they had completely misunderstood Jesus and the figure in which he spoke to them. They are preoccupied with bread, but he spoke of the "yeast" of his religious opponents. They had witnessed his two "bread miracles" earlier in the gospel narrative, but they could not connect his actions and the teaching he offered. Given their pathetic imagination he scolds them yet again:

> *You of little faith, why are you talking about having no bread? Do you still not perceive? Do you not remember the five loaves for the five thousand, and how many baskets you gathered? Or the seven loaves for the four thousand and how many baskets you gathered? How could you fail to perceive that I was not speaking about bread?* (vv. 8-11)

The narrative concludes with this laconic comment:

> *Then they understood that he had not told them to beware of the yeast of bread, but of the teaching of the Pharisees and Sadducees.* (v. 12)

Better late than never!

In all four cases the "little faith" of the disciples is evident because they were preoccupied with the world immediately in front of them: food and clothing, wind and storm, and lack of bread. Their "little faith" and preoccupation with immediate matters caused their pathetic imagination to miss the point about trust in the capacity of God—and more specifically the capacity of Jesus—to provide what is needed for life. Consequently, their little faith caused them to miss out on the chance to trust Jesus and engage on behalf of the coming kingdom of God. The disciples were as limited in their imagination as was the aide to Elisha before them.

Pathetic imagination is the assumption that the world immediately in front of us is the only world on offer. Thus, all possible futures are contained within present observable social reality. This in effect means that there are no alternatives to what we have before us, and so no chance for change, no offer of alternative, no possibility of newness. Those who benefit from the world the way it is presently arranged have a great stake in the claim that this is the only possible world:

- Predatory capitalism likes to claim that the deep inequality between haves and have nots is inevitable. It readily misrepresents the words of Jesus: "You always have the poor with you."
- White supremacists can readily claim that racial superiority and racial inferiority are part of the "natural order" and cannot be altered and so must not be altered.
- Those who benefit from aggressive nationalism prefer to think that war is inevitable, and we must always be over-spending and making preparation for war, because it is sure to come.

Thus, concerning capitalism, racism, and war-mongering nationalism, plus a host of other issues, pathetic imagination serves to maintain the status quo on the assumption that present reality is beyond mutation. Against that, prophetic imagination can see that present social reality is a construction; it can be deconstructed and reconstructed differently for that reason. That is why, against the intransigent chaplains of the status quo, prophetic imagination always asserts that "the days are coming" when an alternative world will emerge among us. For good reason, there are dreamers and there are killers of the dreams!

Such pathetic imagination leads to the domestication of social possibility that limits options for the future. Such domestication in turn invites conformity, because the only way to get ahead is to go along. And such conformity eventually leads to resignation and despair, as we conclude that present reality is our durable fate.

Of course such pathetic imagination readily impacts the church. It is easy enough for a local congregation to assume that what it sees before it is all there can be. Such a view limits vision, curbs energy, and shrivels missional engagement. We frequently played out the drama of domestication and conformity in the local congregation in St. Louis, where I worshiped for a very long time. Whenever we were ready to take a new missional initiative, "George," an older congregation member, always stood up to say, "Be careful; the boiler might go out and require a big payment." His cautionary word was designed to dissuade the congregation from engaging in any bold imagination, action, or expenditure. In the end, such pathetic imagination not only limits the missional energy of the congregation. Eventually, it will and does curb the proclamation of the gospel, so that the church's proclamation is limited to the specificities in front of us. Moreover, domestication can skew the congregation's prayers to be timid and anemic, not daring to sound either bold petition or insistent protest to God. It is no wonder that the state, the church, and society more generally always want to "kill the prophets" because the prophets continue to remind us that the world in front of us is not the only world available to us. Such prophetic imagination intends to deconstruct our present world and construct a new one. For some, that work of deconstruction and reconstruction is emancipatory. For many others, that work must be resisted. It is no wonder that Elijah, the most representative prophet in ancient Israel, was termed by King Ahab to be a "troubler of Israel" (2 Kings 18:17). Prophetic imagination always troubles; pathetic imagination, to the contrary, submits to present reality and never disturbs.

18

HOE! HOE! HOE!

IF YOU MISTAKENLY think this title is a greeting from Santa Claus, then consider this biblical text:

> *Now there was no smith to be found throughout all the land of Israel; for the Philistines said, "The Hebrews must not make swords or spears for themselves"; so all the Israelites went down to the Philistines to sharpen their plowshare, mattocks* ['eth], *axes, or sickles. The charge was two-thirds of a shekel for the plowshares and for the mattocks, and one-third of a shekel for sharpening the axes and for setting the goads. So on the day of the battle neither sword nor spear was to be found in the possession of any of the people with Saul and Jonathan; but Saul and his son Jonathan had them.*
> (1 Samuel 13:19–22)

This remarkable text describes an economy in which the Philistines controlled "the means of production," and the Israelites were left vulnerable and dependent upon the Philistines. The Philistines deliberately maintained a monopoly on the skills and practice of a blacksmith. That posed a great burden upon the Israelites who, as peasant farmers, needed their agricultural tools serviced to produce crops and so to produce a livelihood. The monopoly of the Philistines was undertaken to prevent the Israelites from having military equipment, but the monopoly extended from military to agricultural equipment. Thus, the Israelites had to pay a nameable amount for the sharpening of every plowshare, mattock, axe, or sickle, and we may readily add "hoe."

You may wonder, as I did, what a "mattock" is. I discovered that it is a tool that has a horizontal blade on one side and a standard axe blade on the other. In my childhood we called them "grub hoes" that we used to dig up unwanted sprouts and bushes. We should not miss the point of the text. The Israelites were peasant farmers who could not own their own means of production. The lack of a blacksmith extended not only to extra expense but also to great inconvenience each time a tool needed attention, especially during busy times such as harvest.

All parties, and certainly covenantal Israel, understood that such ironwork as plowshares, mattocks, axes, and sickles, while being agricultural tools, could readily be transformed into spears and swords as weapons of war. Conversely, they also understood that weapons of war, like swords and spears, could be promptly converted into agricultural tools. Thus in the most familiar prophetic poem:

> *They shall beat their swords into plowshares* ['eth],
> *and their spears into pruning hooks;*
> *nation shall not lift up sword against nation,*
> *neither shall they learn war any more.* (Isaiah 2:4; see Micah 43)

Or conversely:

> *Beat your plowshares* ['eth] *into swords,*
> *and your pruning hooks into spears;*
> *let the weakling say, "I am a warrior."* (Joel 3:10)

Also of interest is the only other use of "mattock" (*'eth*) in the Old Testament in 2 Kings 6:1–10. In his preoccupation with the needs of peasants, Elisha came upon a workman, surely a peasant, whose "axe head" (*'eth*) had slipped off the handle and into the water. Elisha retrieves the axe head for the workman, who was helpless and vulnerable without his tool. Thus, Elisha performs one of his acts of restoration and rehabilitation for the peasant community. The recurring theme of all of these uses of "mattock" (*'eth*) is that it is a tool useful for and appropriate to *peasant labor and production.*

It is not, I suggest, a great surprise that this narrative of 1 Samuel 13:19–22 does not occur in the Common Lectionary of the church and is never read in church. Of course, it would not be heard in church as long as the church holds to the uncritical notion that its "good news" concerns spiritual life, the saving of "souls," and the other-worldly afterlife of saved souls. Our narrative obviously has nothing to do with such matters. If, however, the church ever broadly recognizes that its proper "news" concerns such matters, then we might hear this text in church. When the church recognizes that the good news concerns the restoration and rehabilitation of a viable creaturely political economy marked by abundance, then this narrative would be heard in church. Such a gospel concerns how creaturely resources are produced, distributed, and consumed for a livable life. That concern, moreover, clearly involves questions of the control of the means of production. Such control of the means of production (in this case, plowshares, mattocks (*'eth*), axes, and sickles) always includes the recognition that such tools can be variously deployed for well-being (as in agriculture) or for destruction (as weapons of war). It belongs to human well-being to have sufficient control over the means of production so that such a choice can be made for a tool or *weapon*. In our narrative, Israel was denied such a choice, with its future to some great extent kept in the hands of the Philistines.

I have taken so long with this intriguing scriptural narrative as a way of introduction to the most important book I have read in a long time, *The Long Land War: The Global Struggle for Occupancy Rights* (2021) by Jo Guldi. The book is long, dense, and carefully documented. This is a slow, discerning account of the social reality of the world economy in which some populations are left without *Lebensraum* and are therefore vulnerable to the will and whim of those who control the land. Much of Guldi's report concerns, in recent times, the work of the Food and Agricultural Organization (FAO) that was linked to the United Nations and that was formed through the impact of the "Rome Consensus" in 1945. The FAO championed land reform and was committed to land redistribution that would permit vulnerable peasant communities a safe place for work, production, and life. The FAO sought a "third way" of reform that refused market exploitation and state dictatorship, believing that ownership of small plots of land under peasant control was a way to peace and productivity. This approach struck some as obsolete and excessively old-fashioned, but it has its continuing champions, among them not least is Wendell Berry.

At the end of her book, Guldi describes two strategies for land redistribution that have been variously effective. She reports on squatters' rights wherein needy displaced populations have occupied and claimed houses and land. Among successful efforts were the squatters' rights practiced in London by troops returning from World War II. In London, this action received widespread public approval and eventually government endorsement:

> *Squatting represented a new form of community that took the laws of land ownership into its own hands.* (343)

This notion of "self-help occupancy" received vigorous and effective support from Ivan Illich and Paulo Freire (347) and was especially championed by John F. C. Turner, so that it came to be regarded as a movement of entrepreneurs (349). In the context of the United States, this effective movement of squatters needs to be read through the narrative of Matt Desmond and his 2016 book, *Evicted*, which details how landowners have refused such squatter's rights.

The second strategy of land redistribution explored by Guldi is "the technique of the map." Of course, our familiar and widely accepted maps are made top-down by owners, explorers, and their powerful patrons. The making of maps has determined patterns of ownership, control, domination, and eventually production and habitation. But such maps are not "given" descriptions of reality. They are in fact social constructions that are designed to legitimate and secure ownership claims. On the contrary, "the technique of the map" in this book shows that other people can redraw maps to exhibit other social interests. Thus, the book reports on the Appalachian Land Ownership Survey conducted by the Highlander Institute in Tennessee (356). Guldi explores the way in which peasant communities could create "a peoples' map" that is drawn by groups (whole villages!) who walk the land and put their findings on "cheap paper." This "participatory research movement" demonstrates that maps can be drawn differently and that social reality can be constituted differently, and so arrived at "from below" and not "from above" as is our common assumption and practice:

> *Critical of expert management as these movements were—and as dedicated to rethinking the developmental process—none of them before the late 1970s had yet begun to reimagine traditional maps of land tenure. The map was, after all, one of the foremost objects of empire, having been a tool of centralized administration and colonial rule since the origins of the cadastral map in sixteenth-century Europe. By the seventeenth century, European maps were helping settlers lay claim to the lands of other peoples around the globe. By the nineteenth century, expert civil engineers and urban planners were using maps to evict poor families from neighborhoods known to house working-class radicals. In 1980, who would have imagined the map could be used to make a radical claim on the state by those traditionally excluded from participation?*
>
> *The indigenous people whose land was claimed by Canada did just that—and the fact that it was they who did so is striking. Of all of the groups of peasants that had lost their land through eviction, displacement, or indebtedness,*

> *the native tribes in North America have experienced the most extreme injustice; repeated incidents of force, fraud, and broken legal contracts. From the early 1970s, tribes in Alberta had noticed overdevelopment and pollution from expanding mining works encroaching on their territory. As they began to look for a way to ask the Canadian government to enforce their rights in order to exclude miners from their territory, they became aware of the power of maps; in government courts, the map was a tool to mandate adherence to property law.* (365)

Guldi notes, concerning such maps:

> *Organizers had realized that even cheap materials could be used in a process that stressed new habits of mind, suited to the inclusion of persons formerly excluded from the institutions of rule.* (369)

Both strategies of *squatting* and *mapping* depended upon the empowerment of powerless people who could take their lives and futures into their own hands. They could refuse to be passive recipients of whatever the "ownership class" offered them. Such strategies both evoked and required "new habits of the mind" to include those long excluded from the institutions of rule. The new process of map-making was a worldwide project. In the United States, it was led especially by John Gaventa, who presided over the Highlander Institute. Reference should be made to his book, *Power and Powerlessness: Quiescence and Rebellion in an Appalachian Valley* (1980), and the *Appalachian Land Ownership Survey*. Gaventa is now the Director of Research at the Institute of Developmental Studies at the University of Sussex. This university program has been at the forefront of land distribution studies and continues its bold, brave work of fostering a new world of social possibility for heretofore powerless people.

The FAO, since it outset, has been committed to empowering peasant farmers to live and care for the land and to make it productive. Specifically, it has been a champion of providing "technology" appropriate to the peasant economy and the land the peasants could farm and make productive. The technology that was most pertinent and effective, it had concluded, was the *hoe*, a modest form of technology suited to the productivity of small plots of land properly managed and cared for:

> *It was the hoe, rather than the tractor, that would transform developing nations, according to Norris Dodd. With its long handle, the hoe allowed the farmer to work standing up, rather than on his hands and knees; the hoe's industrial steel tongue meant it would last longer than wooden implements. Cheap to manufacture and export, the steel hoe was a symbol of a developmental program that might see poor people manufacturing their own implements, turning farms into factories. Farmers, in other words, would become heralds of a future that was simultaneously industrial and rural.* (131)

Led by Norris Dodd, the FAO was to provide,

> *An information pipeline, connecting peasants of the developing world to small technologies—such as hoes and buckets—and to scientific advice.* (220)

To some extent the work of E. F. Schumacher would continue that passion for simple technology, though Schumacher pushed toward "pump, plow, and modern trucks" to supplement the hoe in a way that pushed toward "development." I have taken this long with Guldi because the FAO's advocacy of "hoes" for peasants to claim land is a powerful, compelling counterpoint to the need for "plowshares, mattocks (*'eth*), axes, and sickles" that concerned ancient Israelites. In both cases such simple technology is a *sine qua non* for the flourishing of a peasant economy and for the good care of the earth. The required submission of the Israelites to Philistine smiths has its contemporary counterpart in the monopoly of technology by the "developed nations" with the World Bank as its vehicle for the maintenance of monopoly and control.

Guldi reports that in the 1970s (the time of the rise of Margaret Thatcher and Ronald Reagan!), the FAO and its advocacy for small peasant farms were overrun by the power of the market, the drive toward industrial agriculture, the consolidation of farmland into even larger farms, and the eradication of the life and culture of small farmers. Thus, we can imagine that the contest between the Philistines and the Israelites over the control of tools was an instance in the ongoing contestation between *industrial bigness* that is committed to growth and the concentration of wealth, and the *peasant practice of modest technology* that precludes big scale and that takes seriously the healthy symbiosis between the land and those who occupy it.

The issues concerning ownership, production, and technology are complex. The resolution of such complexity cannot be reached through scripture study. But scripture study may be a way of framing, or reframing, that contestation. The church's perennial preoccupation with spiritual, soul-saving, other-worldly afterlife plays into the hands of bigness, because such an accent is an abdication of what we know. For that reason, we may well engage in the contestation of scripture . . . whether scripture is to be voiced in the cause of spiritual-soul-other worldly, afterlife or whether the Bible is a voice of advocacy for real-world concerns of production, distribution, consumption, and the force of ownership. The lack of blacksmiths in the peasant economy of ancient Israel consigned Israelites to a relationship of economic dependence, a dependence that continues to be fostered through sharecroppers, tenants, and slaves. The battles joined against the Philistines in subsequent chapters of 1 Samuel constitute a struggle for ownership and control of the means of production. And suppose we accept the hypothesis of Norman Gottwald concerning a "peasant revolt" in ancient Israel. In that case, we can see the significance of the way in which the belated son of Jesse, David, could defeat the Philistine "giant" (1 Samuel 17:1–54). David is not, it turns out, impressed with the bigness of the giant, not the giant of the Philistines who demanded and dictated dependence. It was not for nothing that this small, unnoticed eighth son of Jesse defeated the giant, even as we now face the giant banks, the giant technologies, or the giant markets. As the FAO understood, everything turns on access to technology, a blacksmith, to have a sharp hoe!

The FAO was committed to hoes. The FAO understood that hoes were tools appropriate to the peasants' economy and geography. Against market forces, the FAO championed hoes. Perhaps the FAO understood that if Israel did not have hoes, it could never have a genuine "hoe down" of singing and dancing elation when the hoes are put down in celebration at harvest. The replacement of "hoes" by machines that never rest and that need never to rest may be more "productive." But such scale is unsustainable, because the human community that relies on hoes can anticipate vibrant hoe downs.

19

DESERVES TO BE PAID!

(Luke 10:7)

CONSIDER THIS RECENT news item:

> *The Labor Department found that Packers employed at least 31 children, ranging in age from 13 to 17, who cleaned dangerous equipment with corrosive cleaners during overnight shifts at three slaughtering and meatpacking facilities: a Turkey Valley Farms plant in Marshall, Minn., and JBS USA plants in Grand Island, Neb., and Worthington, Minn.*
>
> *Their jobs included cleaning kill floors, meat- and bone-cutting saws, grinding machines and electric knives, according to court documents. The mix of boys and girls were not fluent English speakers and were interviewed mostly in Spanish, investigators said.*
>
> *The Labor Department found that several minors employed by the company, including one 13-year-old, suffered caustic chemical burns and other injuries. One14-year-old boy, who worked from 11 p.m. to 5 a.m. five to six days a week, suffered injuries from chemical burns for cleaning machines used to cut meat. School records showed that the student fell asleep in class or missed class because of the job at the plant. (Remy Tumin, "Labor Dept. Finds 31 Minors Employed in Meat Plants,"* New York Times, *November 12, 2022, B6)*

In Minnesota and Nebraska, for God's sake!

By happenstance, I read two books back-to-back that seemed to have no connection to each other. To my surprise the two books converged around the issue of the exploitation of labor. The first of these books is *Of Blood and Sweat: Black Lives and the Making of White Power and Wealth* (2022) by Clyde Ford. The thesis and argument of the book is that Black labor (as slaves, tenant farmers, sharecroppers, or later low-wage workers) constitutes the source of white wealth:

> *From slavery in the seventeenth century to the designation of "essential workers" in the time of the pandemic in the twenty-first century, the essential elements of racial interaction in America have not changed: Black lives are a means to an end for all too many White Americans. That end? Greater wealth. To protect the acquisition of greater wealth? Greater power.* (p. 6)

Ford sees and voices clearly the dialectic of white freedom and Black bondage:

> *Freedom from slavery threatened the freedom of White planters. Said another way: white planters and slave owners realized their freedom was tied to the bondage of their slaves.* (p. 81)

This combination of *benefit* and *exploitation* was written into US law. Beyond that, Ford judges that much of the US Constitution is preoccupied with the preservation of white domination and assurance of Black subservience:

> *The total number of clauses within the Constitution varies somewhere between 75 and 85, depending upon what is, or is not, considered a clause. That means a staggering amount of the Constitution, between 20 to 25 percent, is devoted directly or indirectly to supporting slavery, and excluding*

> *Black Americans from the benefits conferred to "We the People."* (155)

As the news item cited above indicates, the exploitation of labor is not confined to Black people. But of course the practice of such exploitation and its long-standing institutionalization are devoted primarily to Black labor.

The other book I read is *The Man Who Broke Capitalism: How Jack Welch Gutted the Heartland and Crushed the Soul of Corporate America—and How to Undo His Legacy* (2022) by David Gelles. The book is a detailed account of the work and career of Jack Welch, the long-time CEO of General Electric. The phrase in the title, "Broke Capitalism," refers to the way in which Welch quite intentionally departed from the conventional, respectful interaction of management and labor, to reduce labor to an inconvenient business expense with workers reduced to the status of the least secure and the most readily dispensable. In the end, Welch had very little interest in product development or in the flourishing of the industry, but was singularly committed to producing profit income for investors.

Welch's ruthless strategy of demeaning and dismissing workers led to massive layoffs, rigorous downsizing, and outsourcing, so that he developed

> *a whole infrastructure [which] had been created to support this liminal state of employment, normalizing economic insecurity. Even at some of the country's largest employers, there is a concerted effort to keep workers as close to temps as they can possibly be, with the aspiration of making people as interchangeable as the parts of a machine.* (169–170)

Specifically, Welch developed a "Vitality Curve" (171) that led managers to "rate" workers, with the intent of firing the lowest 10 percent of the workforce each year. He does so to bring in new workers, dispose of the least productive, and create a work environment of anxiety, in which workers had to compete with each other, thus developing a work culture of unwillingness to help one another at all.

Before he finishes, Gelles adds a report on work policy at Amazon under Jeff Bezos, who finds coercive ways to replicate and advance the policies of Welch. At Amazon, workers are taken to be "fundamentally expendable" and must always live with the threat of dismissal (171–172). Thus, workers at Amazon

> *are subjected to ever more dystopian forms of management, where people are treated like machines, workplace injuries are common, and any vestige of sentimentality is snuffed out.* (172)

The matter is not different, Gelles insists, at Starbucks, for example:

> *Companies like Starbucks have put workers on call for shifts that could be canceled at the last minute. Hourly employees have been scheduled to work the late shift, then open the same restaurant the next morning on just a few hours of sleep, a practice known as "clopening."* (170)

This pattern of exploitation is reiterated whenever a large corporation has an interest only in the bottom line of profitability for shareholders to the neglect of everything and everyone else.

Happily, Gelles is able to report at the end of his book that in more recent times there are more "enlightened" corporate managers who have rejected the Welch–Bezos–Schultz model of exploitation and have returned to a more humane recognition of workers as essential to the well-being and long-term wealth of a company.

When we juxtapose Ford's review of Black labor and Gelles's articulation of recent corporate practice, it is easy enough to see defining continuities between the two. In both cases the aim is immediate and immense profit for owners-managers. In both cases the requirement for such profit-making is that workers are dispensable and can be treated on the cheap, with no right or claim of their own. It is obvious that the news cited above from the meat-packing industry is in continuity with Jack Welch's vision of dispensable labor and with the older, long-running violence and exploitation of slavery and Jim Crow culture.

It cannot be unimportant to the church, as to the synagogue, that the long-running story of God's engagement with the human economy begins in the narrative of a labor dispute. That labor dispute is articulated in the narrative of Exodus 5 that sounds like a harbinger of the US slave economy and the later US corporate economy via Welch or Bezos.

In the Exodus narrative Pharaoh's work policy is simply to increase the production schedule and force his slave workers to greater effort:

> *You shall no longer give the people straw to make bricks, as before; let them go and gather straw for themselves. But you shall require of them the same quantity of bricks as they have made previously; do not diminish it, for they are lazy; that is why they cry, "Let us go and offer sacrifice to our God" . . . He said, "You are lazy, lazy; that is why you say, "Let us go and sacrifice to the Lord." Go now, and work; for no straw shall be given you, but you shall deliver the same number of bricks."* (Exodus 5:7–8, 17–18)

So at Amazon:

> *Workers who just clocked fifty-five-hour weeks can suddenly be assigned mandatory overtime, with no one to appeal to. Sometimes, the algorithm accidentally fires workers, who, despite begging to remain employed with the company, are out of a job. Cameras and computers are watching Amazon*

> *employees every minute of the day. Workers on the warehouse floor are tracked constantly, with sensors recording how fast they pack boxes and how long they linger, perhaps catching their breath. Time spent using the bathroom can result in lower performance reviews. Any lag in productivity is assumed to be the fault of a lazy worker. Drivers have resorted to peeing in bottles, and factory workers who walk too slowly have been disciplined.* (The Man Who Broke Capitalism, 172–173)

Where the ancient Hebrew slaves wanted time off to worship (that is, to rendezvous with the emancipatory God), workers at Amazon might want a break for rest.

> *We are human beings. We are not tools used to make their daily/weekly goals and rates.* (173)

It goes without saying that such ruthless exploitative policies help to produce great wealth for management and shareholders. Thus, we see on exhibit the economic wealth of Bezos, Elon Musk, and their ilk, as well as the major shareholders who support and insist upon cheap labor. It is the rule here as it was in ancient Egypt or under Jim Crow: *cheap labor begets great wealth.*

It is clear in the Old Testament that the fantastic wealth of King Solomon derived from the cheap labor of slaves. We have one direct and immediate prophetic charge against the royal house for its systemic exploitation of labor, though many other prophetic utterances tilt with the same awareness. In his condemnation of King Jehoiakim (*Shallum*), the prophet Jeremiah addresses the issue directly:

> *Woe . . . [big trouble to come!—]*
> *to him who builds his house by unrighteousness,*

> *and his upper rooms by injustice;*
> *who makes his neighbors work for nothing,*
> *and does not give them their wages.* (Jeremiah 22:13)

The king specializes in "not-righteousness" and in "not-justice." He requires his "neighbors" to work for nothing. He withholds their wages. The use of the term "neighbor" is surely intended in an ironic, puckish way, to remind the king and his company that his exploited workers are his "neighbors," members of the fabric of the neighborhood, and not intruders from outside or strangers to the common enterprise of living together. The use of the term "neighbor" suggests a vulnerability that bespeaks mutual obligation. But exploitative management always seeks to banish the notion of social solidarity with labor, all the way from Pharaoh to Judean kings, to Jim Crow, to current corporate policy. Once "neighboring" is eliminated, every means of exploitation becomes available.

It is amazing that in his compilation of Torah commandments in the book of Deuteronomy, Moses takes the trouble to think of exploited neighbors. While preoccupied with holy sites, holy foods, and holy festivals, Moses pauses long enough to think about the economy. Among the "miscellaneous" commandments concerning the economy, Moses commands this:

> *You shall not withhold the wages of poor and needy laborers, whether Israelites or aliens who reside in your land in one of your towns. You shall pay them their wages daily before sunset, because they are poor and their livelihood depends on them; otherwise they might cry to the Lord against you, and you would incur guilt.* (Deuteronomy 24:14–15)

Moses understood, as does every number-crunching manager, that profits depend on the minute control of cash flow. Thus, it is profitable to withhold payment for a day or a week and put the money to other gainful use. But "no," says Moses! The worker is entitled to their pay. The worker, whether an Israelite or an outsider (immigrant), whether a kinsman or an outsider, has entitlement. It is recognized in the commandment that vulnerable daily workers are poor; they always are. Our translation speaks of their "livelihood" that depends on such prompt payment. The Hebrew term is "*nephesh*," thus their life, their self-hood, their existence depends on prompt payment. If not paid promptly, such a worker might "cry to the Lord"; the phrase would have evoked in Israel an Exodus memory. It was the cry of the slaves in Egypt (Exodus 2:23–25) that evoked the emancipatory God to action that undid the Pharaonic system. Thus, in the Torah-horizon of Moses, such a small economic transaction between owner and worker becomes a *cosmic issue* that concerns the creator of heaven and earth. The outcome cannot be good for such a parsimonious owner. The matter is reflected in the wise saying of Israel:

> *Those who mock the poor insult their Maker.* (Proverbs 17:5)

There is no more effective or dangerous way to mock the poor than to withhold payment. Such a mocking evokes the creator God, just as the mocking of the poor Hebrew slaves by Pharaoh evoked that emancipatory God to act.

We may take this single commandment from Moses as a signal that Israel's Torah is exactly and explicitly "invested" in the well-being of the workers. This single rule of prompt payment may be construed as a hint of a host of workers' rights that are not to be disregarded by owners and managers. Thus, it is all of a piece:

- the slavery of Pharaoh,
- the exploitation by Israelite and Judean kings,
- the ruthless habits of US slavery and Jim Crow,

- the contemporary ruthlessness of corporations that reduces workers to dispensable cogs in a profit-making machine, and
- the sweatshops of meatpacking companies in Nebraska and Minnesota.

We in the church might take a deep breath to reflect on the long-running, systemic ways in which we have screened out what matters as theological issues. We have, over a long period of time, opted for safer theological issues more remote from life, to the neglect of these issues deeply rooted in the Torah. We have indeed chosen badly where our energy might best be directed:

> *Woe to you, scribes and Pharisees, hypocrites! For you tithe mint, dill, and cummin, and have neglected the weightier matters of the Torah; justice, and mercy and faith. It is these you ought to have practiced without neglecting the others.* (Matthew 23:23)

What is needed is not charity for workers. What is required are good laws and regulations that concern the well-being and welfare of workers who are, at the outset, without social power. Thus, we may usefully spend some energy on this question: What is possible by way of policy and practice for the sake of workers in Marshall, Grand Island, and Worthington and everywhere that workers are exploited and maltreated? It is evident that this matter of justice for workers is further skewed by racism, as the divide between owners/managers and workers is further skewed along racial lines. In the long run, it is a question of whether the sovereignty of God pertains to our common life in the world. If it does, much follows for public policy and public practice. If it does not, then it matters not at all.

There is a fairly straight line from the *commandment of Moses* (Deuteronomy 24:15–16) to the *oracle of Jeremiah* (Jeremiah 22:13) to the *parable of Jesus* concerning pay for workers (Matthew 20:1–10). It is noticeable and disconcerting that the parable of Jesus ends with the unnerving assurance:

> *So the last will be first, and the first will be last.*
> (Matthew 20:16)

The gospel is uncompromising in its insistence on the good future of "the least"!

20

CITIES OF REFUGE?

FROM OF OLD the land of Canaan had an economy organized in exploitative ways. This economy was a tributary system whereby the wealth produced by agricultural peasants trickled up to the numerous "city-states" and their "city-kings." The city-states were governed by "kings" whose authority reached as far into the hinterland as their power allowed. The result was an enriched, empowered "urban elite" clustered around the king and benefited from wealth that trickled up. The "downside" of such trickle-up in a tributary system is that the agricultural peasants survived on a subsistence level, not enjoying the benefit of their produce. This arrangement was considered "normal" as long as the city-kings prevailed.

That system, however, was severely and effectively challenged by a revolt among the peasants. That revolt, legitimated and authorized by YHWH, the Lord of emancipation, turned out to be the emergence of the covenantal community of Israel that worked to overthrow the Canaanite tributary system. Over time "Israel"—the peasant revolt—gained ground and took control of more and more territory, even though the Israelite scriptures honestly report that in many places the covenantal peasants "did not drive out" the Canaanites. (Note that repeated refrain in Judges 1:27–33.)

The transfer of land away from *the tributary system* to *a covenantal arrangement* is reported in the two great interpretive traditions of ancient Israel, the Priestly and the Deuteronomic. While these two traditions contain much later imaginative material from the time of their writing, it is credible to conclude that they also contain authentic memories of the time of the "land transfer." In these two interpretive traditions it is clear that Israel not only seized control of some of the land, but that Israel intended that the land (now "the land of promise") should be organized and managed very differently. The Priestly tradition intends (and remembers) that the land is to be newly organized in order to maintain the *holiness* of Israel that is commensurate with the *holiness* of YHWH:

> *You shall be holy, for I the Lord your God am holy.* (Leviticus 19:2)

Conversely, the Deuteronomic tradition intends (and remembers) that the newly acquired land is to be organized around neighborly *justice* that is commensurate with YHWH's will for *justice:*

> *Justice, and only justice, you shall pursue, so that you may live and occupy the land that the Lord your God is giving you.* (Deuteronomy 16:20)

For good reason these two interpretive traditions diverge from each other in quite remarkable ways, given their very different interests and agenda. Consequently, they offer two very different versions of the character of Israel and of the intent of YHWH, the Lord of the peasant revolt.

However, both interpretive traditions stress that the covenantal administration of the land (now "of promise") is to be quite in contrast to the predatory ways of the Canaanite tributary system. My purpose here is to call attention to the fact that both interpretive traditions, for all their difference, advocate for and legitimate a most remarkable practice, namely, the designation of "cities of refuge." In the Priestly tradition, the founding of "cities of refuge" is carefully delineated (Numbers 35:9–28). The text provides for six such cities to which a person may flee for protection if that person has caused an accidental death:

> *But if someone pushes another suddenly without enmity, or hurls any object without lying in wait, or, while handling any stone that could cause death, unintentionally drops it on another and death ensues, though they were not enemies and no harm was intended, then the congregation shall judge between the slayer and the avenger of blood, in accordance with these ordinances; and the congregation shall rescue the slayer from the avenger of blood. Then the congregation shall send the slayer back to the original city of refuge.* (vv. 22–25)

These verses are in the context of a prospect for swift, severe punishment for anyone who is a murderer. But noteworthy is the care taken to protect the innocent who are vulnerable in a society that is fiercely bent toward vengeance and retaliation. Such a person receives protection from the community to be kept safe from unwarranted vengeance and violence.

The same provision is offered in Deuteronomy 19:1–9 (see also 4:41–43). The place of safe refuge is on offer for someone who "unintentionally" kills another person when there is no enmity between them. This provision on the lips of Moses lines out an illustrative case in point:

> *Suppose someone goes into the forest with another to cut wood, and when one of them swings the ax to cut down a tree, the head slips from the handle and strikes the other person who then dies; the killer may flee to one of these cities and live.* (v. 5)

As is characteristic in Deuteronomy, the specific practice is linked to the wider community in two ways. First, this specific requirement of cities of refuge is linked to the larger covenantal norm of Deuteronomy:

> *provided you diligently observe this entire commandment that I command you today, by loving the Lord your God and walking always in his ways.* (v.9)

Second, the concern of the provision, in the end, is not the protection of an individual, but rather the purity of the land, that it not be polluted by "bloodguilt":

> *So that the blood of an innocent person may not be shed in the land that the Lord your God is giving you as an inheritance, whereby bringing bloodguilt upon you.* (v. 10)

In this Deuteronomic commandment, as in Numbers 35 in the Priestly tradition, this provision for cities of refuge is in the context of fierce judgment against intentional killing:

> *Show no pity; you shall purge the guilt of innocent blood from Israel, so that it may go well with you.* (v. 13)

Thus, in both interpretive traditions, provision is made for "cities of refuge" that protect the innocent who are vulnerable. A third reference to such cities of refuge is voiced in Joshua 20:1–9 that brings the subject closer to Joshua's control of the land in Israel's narrative memory. In quite concrete ways, Israelite "land management" is very different from that of the exploitative Canaanite system that offered no chance to participate in a neighborly covenant, had no interest in protecting the vulnerable, and was not worried about "bloodguilt" violating the land. Thus, the subsistence peasants who reordered the land in covenantal ways had in purview more than the protection of wealth. They had in mind a viable neighborly community in which the neighbors looked out for each other, especially looking out for the vulnerable who had no resources to protect themselves.

It may indeed be that both commandments that set aside cities of refuge are not more than visionary acts of imagination that were not implemented in reality. We do not know, but we do know that Israel's constituent character led to such a visionary possibility that refused to give in to the predatory practices of the antecedent Canaanite exploitative economic system. We note, moreover, that this visionary possibility is not an appeal to charity or goodwill; it is a matter of a Torah commandment that is constituent of a covenantal community. It is commanded! No doubt there were those who insisted that real estate, especially urban real estate, is too valuable to use up in such a generous way. The Torah, however, is insistent and uncompromising in its protection of the vulnerable, even if that protection requires the appropriation of valuable real estate to be utilized for such protective policies.

The interpretive extrapolations we might make from these Torah provisions are rather obvious. The lesson of these two pieces of Torah is that the covenantal community, as a community of neighbors, has an obligation to make specific and generous provisions for our vulnerable neighbors who are at the mercy of an exploitative economic system. To test the urgency of such provision in our own time and place, we need only make an inventory of all the vulnerable among us who lack the means of self-protection. This list is familiar to us:

women
children and young people
old people
people of color
gay people
disabled people
immigrants
poor people

This is the list of people, via "race, class, and gender," who live outside the *protective hegemony of white males.*

The predatory system of American capitalism is something of a rough parallel to the exploitative system of ancient Canaan. In both cultural constructs, there is a trickle-up of wealth based and reliant on the practice of cheap labor. The *theological* question of neighborliness becomes the *economic* question of how resources are to be allocated to provide protection, security, dignity, and well-being for the vulnerable who too often bear the "stigma" of being "unproductive." One does not need to be a "liberal" or a "progressive" to conclude from these Torah provisions that the resources of the community must be organized for such protective initiatives as cities of refuge.

In my hometown we have a "shelter" for people whom we designated as "homeless." It is called Safe Harbor; Safe Harbor is a night shelter during the cold months for as many as one hundred and twenty people. It is backed and staffed by volunteers, church people and others. Our church's part of this effort is led by the indefatigable intrepid Jane Lippert who brings her wisdom, passion, and energy every day to the task in which she is joined by many others. It is a specific refuge of care, but it is minimal for people who lack resources and who are vulnerable on many counts. It is inadequate for our community. What is needed and required is a broad-based public policy that accepts responsibility for all the neighbors, that is properly financed, and that is administered with generative, compassionate attentiveness. We designate the guests at Safe Harbor as "homeless." But we might do better to refer to such needful people as "displaced" people, as people who have no "place" of safety and well-being in the larger community that is geared to the "productive" who contribute to the common good of the community. To be "dis-placed"—that includes all those in the inventory just above—is to have no place of belonging. These Torah provisions offer such people a "place" of safety and well-being. On reading these Torah texts, we might pay attention to the many different ways in which people in our society are displaced, living without a safe place. And we might consider how it is that such people who are our neighbors may come to a safe place, that is, to a Safe Harbor.

But, of course, the predatory system of Canaan has a long, durable shelf life in "the land of promise." The exploitative ways of Canaan (overcome in part by Israelite covenantalism) continued to be available among the Israelites. It is for sure that Israel "did not drive out" Canaanite ways and Canaanite assumptions. Those ways and assumptions lingered amid Israel's covenantalism. It is evident, moreover, that Canaanite ways were soon reiterated by the monarchy of Solomon, who is perhaps the greatest "Canaanite city-king" who was completely committed to the usurpatious ways of Canaan. (Thus, see 1 Kings 10:14–22 on Solomon's avarice.) In 1 Kings 2, we are told that Solomon seized for himself the royal throne in violent ways and without the luxury of public acclamation. His ascent to power was an inside job accomplished through ruthless violence. On his way to the throne he followed the counsel of his father David and killed Shimei, who had cursed the king:

> *Then the king commanded Benaiah son of Jehoiada; and he went out and struck him down, and he died.* (I Kings 2:46)

In like manner he disposed of his brother Adonijah, who was his rival for the throne.

> *So Solomon sent Benaiah son of Jehoiada; he struck him down, and he died.* (1 Kings 2:25)

But the most illuminating episode of such violence on the way to power concerns Joab, the faithful military commander of David. David had, in ironically careful ways, instructed Solomon to do away with Joab:

> *Act therefore according to our wisdom, but do not let his gray head go down to Sheol in peace.* (v. 6)

Fearful for his life,

> *Joab fled to the tent of the Lord and grasped the horn of the altar.* (v. 28)

The altar was the final and most secure "safe harbor" for the vulnerable who could not protect themselves. Solomon, nonetheless, is unblinking in his violent determination and does not hesitate. He accuses Joab of bloodguilt concerning Abner and Amasa, two deaths that Joab accomplished in his loyalty to David. Solomon readily issues one more death sentence. He orders his hatchet-man, Benaiah, to seize Joab from the altar. Benaiah willingly obeys his would-be king:

> *Then Benaiah son of Jehoiada went up and struck him down and killed him. And he was buried at his own house near the wilderness.* (v. 34)

This action of Solomon and Benaiah is nothing less than the invasion of a place of safe security. (The reiterated death sentence at the hands of Benaiah sounds not unlike the parade of ruthless violence in the vendetta of *The Godfather*.) It would be like intruding violently into a city of refuge. Or invasion into a Safe Harbor. There is no safe place from the aggression of avarice, Canaanite or capitalist, for the vulnerable who lack the means and resources for protection. It turned out that even in Israel, no one was safe from the shameless drive to seize control and exercise domination.

In a lesser maneuver, Solomon declined to kill the priest who had backed his rival for the throne; Solomon exiled the long-running high priest of David, Abiathar (1 Kings 2:26–27). In his act of exile, he puts the old priest on notice:

> *I will not at this time put you to death.* (v. 26)

The phrasing "at this time" must have endlessly echoed in the heart and mind of the old priest. If not now, then when?

Taken in sum, these several actions of Solomon, narrated in sober repetition, let us see in the tradition of Israel the continuing contestation between two economic systems, one that provides protective care for the vulnerable and the other that will stop at nothing on its violent way to wealth, power, and control. That deep contradiction runs through the flow of biblical tradition. And of course it runs through our own contemporary life. There is an exploitative system of economics that is powerful in our public life that subordinates all else to the greater accumulation of money and power. That system receives political and legal cover from the leverage and control that such greed exercises in our political life. This system's seizures of the vulnerable are slower, less obvious, and less dramatic than that done by Solomon and Benaiah. But the outcomes are too often the same, the doing in of the vulnerable. Alongside that powerful enterprise is a countertheme of shared well-being that includes the generous economy of a neighborly community. The tension between the two is fierce and unending, and the forces of concentrated money and resolved greedy power always seem to prevail. But the ancient provision for "cities of refuge" witnesses to an alternative. It is the alternative that must be re-engaged and re-embraced among us. That is the proper business of the covenanted community, the proper engagement of the church. The predatory system is always seizing vulnerable people from safe places and displacing them. But the old advocacy of the Torah for otherwise persists. And we church people are among its heirs, heirs who continue to provide safe places and resist the predatory power that still echoes the old Canaanite city-kings. We may indeed wonder: *Why is it that these verses are never heard in church?*

21

TAKE TWENTY!

ONE SUMMER IN high school I painted barns with "Uncle Billy" Cook and his son, Raymond. We worked long days six days a week. My arm felt like it would fall off. As tired as I was, my dad gave me some good, concrete advice: "Drink a rest." Take a long, slow walk to get a drink of water. Sip it slowly and make it last. Make it very slow so that you can get some rest.

I thought of this good advice concerning rest as I read the amazing account of slave society in the Old South by Clint Smith, *How the Word Is Passed: A Reckoning with the History of Slavery across America* (2021). Among the matters Smith reports on is an old well on Pearl Street:

> *A block of bricks that jutted up from the sidewalk, with a golden ring encircling a well that was covered in grass. I looked over the rails and into this hole in the ground and saw deteriorating bricks covered in algae, small plants reaching from one side of the cistern to the other.* (218)

The well dated back to the eighteenth century and served the community in a special way:

> *The first and final thing an enslaved person did every day was get water from the well for their households, and it was here that they were able to spend time together. "You were allowed to look that person in the eyes," Damaras said. "You were allowed do say 'Good morning.' The enslaved people who*

> *came to this well," she continued, "were able to reclaim their humanity for just twenty minutes out of their day."*

Smith concludes:

> *They were human at the well, and they were human away from it.*

Time at the well each day with their friends provided moments of well-being outside of and beyond the hard days of coerced labor. The slaved did indeed "drink a rest" from their "normal" day's work of unrelieved bondage. This moment of "humanity" must have kept alive social possibility and communal hope that their lives were not finally defined by or contained within the endless cruelty of enslavement.

It is amazing how a watering-place or a village well can be a site for human communication, human community, human well-being, and human restoration. That process of recovery and rehabilitation, regularly reiterated, lasted only "twenty minutes out of their day." Those twenty minutes, however, were sufficient to conjure an alternative life in an emancipated community.

With my dad's advice about "drinking a rest" and Smith's account of "twenty minutes out of their day," I thought of "gatherings at the village well" in Scripture. The primary case in point I consider is from one of my favorite passages. In the Song of Deborah (Judges 5:1–31) Israel celebrates a mighty victory over its Canaanite adversaries. The conflict featured the poorly armed Israelite subsistence peasant farmers (see 1 Samuel 13:19–22) against the well-armed kings of Canaanite city-states. The conflict turned on the ruthless capacity of the city-kings to siphon off the surplus wealth of the peasant farmers for their own advantage and indulgence. (In this regard the socio-economic situation of the peasant farmers was not unlike that of the much later slaves in the plantation South who had the product of their labor siphoned off for white surplus and advantage. In cases, the productive class (peasant farmers, slaves) was helpless before the armed power of the "master class."

Thus, the assertion of power by Israelite peasant farmers was against very long odds. All the more reason to have the victory celebrated! The victory song gladly credits the triumph to the "new God" (YHWH), newly arrived from the Exodus and unknown to the Canaanites (V. 6). This is the creator God who could mobilize the stars and the flood waters on behalf of Israel:

The kings came, they fought;
then fought the kings of Canaan,
at Taanach, by the waters of Megiddo;
they got no spoils of silver.
The stars fought from heaven,
from their courses they fought against Sisera.
The torrents of Kishon swept them away,
the onrushing torrent, the torrent Kishon.
March on my soul with might! (vv. 19–21)

At the same time the victory song is glad to credit the crucial contribution of the Israelite tribes to the victory, led by Deborah and Barak (vv. 12–15). The song celebrates the heroism of Jael, an Israelite woman who confounded (and murdered) the Canaanite general, Sisera (vv. 24–27). The song, syllable by syllable, lines out the dramas of Sisera's last moments at the hand of the brave Israelite woman:

He sank, he fell,
He lay still at her feet;
at her feet he sank, he fell,
where he sank, there he fell dead. (v. 27)

Perhaps the community would engage in a chanting recital of these cadences. So giddy is the joy of Israel that the poetry can even imagine the pathos of the mother of the Canaanite general as she figured out that her son—the general—is dead in battle and is not coming home (vv. 28–30).

What interests me just now is the remarkable interlude in the poem in verses 10–11:

Tell of it, you who ride on white donkeys,
you who sit on rich carpets,
and you who walk by the way.
To the sound of musicians at the watering places,
there they repeat the triumphs of the Lord,
the triumphs of his peasantry in Israel.

These verses readily recognize the most likely social venue where the victory of Israel will be endlessly recited. The first line of these verses begins with three participles concerning those who ride, those who sit, and those who walk, that is, everybody! Only at the end of the line do we get the verb "tell!" Speak out loud. Break the silence with exuberance!

And then we get the venue for such "telling." The watering places! Go to the village well; meet the other women. Linger, and then sing and dance, all to the beat of the musicians. We can imagine that the village well was the most likely venue with the women, the children and their dogs gathering for a few minutes of respite, singing and dancing, from the hard labor of subsistence farming. The poem of Deborah, moreover, gives the women at the well the ground for their singing and dancing. The song never grows old; it is an act of defiance against present economic reality. The two lines give us the topic in poetic parallelism. In the first line the theme is "the triumphs of YHWH." The song is about YHWH, the creator God, the new God from the exodus, achieving an unimaginable victory over well-armed Canaanite forces. Sing that wondrous impossibility! The second line, in perfect poetic parallelism, credits the same "triumph" to the peasants of Israel. It was their bravery that won the day! Thus, the victory is credited, in turn, to YHWH and to the peasants. But this is poetry. The singing women do not need to sort out the parallelism or to parse it with precision. It is a victory for both YHWH and the peasants, who colluded to accomplish this mighty historical upset. There is no offer of explanation. There is only singing acknowledgment. The term rendered "triumphs," moreover, is *sidqoth*, a feminine plural noun from the root term *sadiq* that we take as "righteousness." Thus, the victory is construed as an act of "making right," a socio-economic circumstance most assuredly skewed and distorted. The predatory practice of the Canaanite city-kings toward the subsistence farmers was not "right." The victory "corrects" an unbearable historical arrangement. The women dance and sing at the village well of the great inexplicable reversal in the circumstance of their life. The poetry does not explain; it lines out the endlessly treasured and reiterated memory.

We can imagine that this singing at the village well was an example of the "hidden transcript" of James C. Scott, *Domination and the Arts of Resistance: Hidden Transcripts* (1990). Scott recognizes that the historically lowly and economically vulnerable have a narrative of lived reality that they recite to each other only in private. It is a narrative to which the overlords can never gain access. And so the women come to the well to exult with each other in the recital of their hidden transcript that gives identity to their communal existence and that defies their status as subservient to the Canaanite city kings.

So let us imagine that they could linger only briefly at the village well, say twenty minutes. It was, as Smith sees later on, twenty minutes in which the Israelite women could recover and reassert their Israelite identity as members of an emancipated covenant community. It was twenty minutes of laughing and telling and singing and dancing whereby they could recover their community identity and their humanity. And the children must have watched and must have inhaled the sweet smell of alternative reality. They learned the hidden transcript of emancipated slaves before they knew it, and they would, later, tell their children. We can imagine that the women, as they were able, never missed a chance to go to the well. They would hobble, crippled to get there. They would stop to go there when they were too old to go. This break at the village well was crucial to their existence and to their day-to-day coping with the demand of the Canaanite city kings.

My reflection on this remarkable scene of reiteration and formation in ancient Israel caused me to think as well of the scene in John 4 where Jesus meets the Samaritan women "at the well." We are told that Jesus went there because he was "tired" (John 4:6). It is not said that he was thirsty, though he likely was. He asked for a drink from the women (v. 7). We are not told why the woman was at the well; she no doubt needed water and was thirsty, but since the Fourth Gospel narrative is thick with freight beyond the obvious, we can take it that she came to the well for respite from her lived reality. After all, she was a Samaritan outsider and she had seven husbands. She must have been a social outcast. But then she belongs to a long company of social outcasts who come to the well for revitalization and recovery of identity.

Thus, I want to consider the convergence of these moments at the village well where a counter-narrative can be reiterated that defies the dominant narrative:

- The Israelite women recited the story of YHWH and the peasants, defying the dominance of the Canaanite city kings.
- The Samaritan woman at the village well received a new story of her life that was on offer nowhere else.
- The Black slaves, on Pearl Street, came to the well for twenty minutes of humanity that kept them emancipated all day long.

In all these instances, the world out beyond the well is endlessly demanding, exploitative, and coercive. Thus, by itself, the world beyond the well will enslave and dehumanize.

- So the Israelites faced the demanding, exploitative, coercive force of the Canaanite city kings . . . and the well provided respite.
- So the Samaritan woman lived in a Jewish society that endlessly reprimanded her for her second-class identity and her failed marital life . . . and the well offered respite.
- So the plantation economy, with its endless cotton quotas, reduced the life of the slaves to labor without possible gain . . . and the well offered respite.

Now consider the insatiable demands of our economy of production and consumption. For those "below," the story features low wages with never enough to maintain life beyond debt. For those "above," there is the endless rat race to have more, to get ahead, to rise higher. The outcome is that those "below" and those "above" share a common pressure propelled by anxiety. Amid such widely shared anxiety with large doses of fear, the dominant society offers little respite, as the sabbath has rendered obsolete as a possible pivot point of well-being. The result, not surprisingly, is a society that is deeply on edge, prone to violence, whether against neighbor or against self (suicide). The dominant narrative provides no escape from the demands for performance.

We may learn from these old examples of a pause at the village well—the peasant community of ancient Israel, the Samaritan women with Jesus, and the slaves of the plantation economy—that we must seek out and have available venues for respite that defy the dominant narrative and that invite to an alternative identity. I asked my favorite doctor, Christina McHugh Brueggemann, MD, what we might learn from medical science about a "twenty-minute" rehabilitation. Here is her most helpful response to me:

> *Many studies have been done over the years that show that at least twenty minutes of exercise daily can greatly reduce cardiovascular risk factors and improve your overall health.*

> *In older adults, it has also been shown to improve cognitive function as well as physical health. In a recent study, elder adults cycled on stationary bikes for twenty minutes, and their post-exercise cognitive functioning showed marked improvement. Especially in areas that involved executive functioning or organizational tasks.*
>
> *Studies have also been done that show the same benefit from taking twenty minutes to do some rest or relaxation techniques such as meditation, or deep breathing. It has been found that people who incorporated daily "brain rest" into their routines had less anxiety, less stress, and even a lowering of their blood pressure. They experienced an improved emotional health and a more positive outlook on life.*
>
> *Some forms of meditation can enhance your self-awareness and can teach you to recognize thoughts that can be harmful or self-defeating. It can also increase your attention span and decrease memory loss. For all these reasons, many physicians (including me!) recommend daily exercise or relaxation/meditation routines for people of all ages.* (private communication)

Neither the women clustered around Deborah at the village well in ancient Israel nor the slaves on Pearl Street at the well nor my dad had any of this scientific data. But they all understood intuitively what Dr. Brueggemann is affirming here. It all comes down to the practice of "twenty minutes" to rehabilitate our humanness that has been abased.

Ray Oldenburg, in *The Great Good Place* (1989), has delineated a requirement for such a "third pace" that is beyond the spheres of family and of work for the work of rehabilitation. Such a "third place" invites "civic engagement" and regeneration of self. The possibility of a third place offers many candidates: the barber shop, bar (*Cheers!*), or library. Of course the church has been, historically, exactly such a third place where an alternative narrative (hidden transcript) could be compellingly reperformed. The church has no monopoly on this indispensable generic social function. But it does provide a quite distinct hidden transcript that has no effective counter-point in any other third place venue. The hidden transcript that powers and funds the church as a third place is put most succinctly in the congregational response in the Eucharist:

> *Christ has died;*
> *Christ is risen;*
> *Christ will come again.*

This is a recital that has no credibility in the dominant world of production and consumption. It is, moreover, a narrative that is not obvious or easy in its claim. Thus, many conservatives take the "come again" of the third line and imagine a dateline. Most progressive Christians, I conclude, mostly mumble over the transcript. If, however, we notice the claim about Lordship that is intrinsic to the recital, it has the effect of rendering penultimate all other claims. Thus, the first Easter narrative was and is a defiance and dismantling of ultimate power of Caesar and the empire of Rome. And now, in our Western economy, the claim has the force of rendering penultimate the claim of the market. We are observing, slowly and belatedly amid Covid, that the market cannot keep its promises and cannot deliver what we most need and want for our lives. That is on offer only elsewhere!

So imagine a church meeting. It may last only twenty minutes, often more. In the long-running tradition of the Black Church, the meeting lasted a very long time, for who could want to rush back to whitey's world? The meeting cannot be rushed. It is a meeting in which a dramatic count-world is on offer and is being reperformed. Because it a "world" and not an argument or a program or a demand, it cannot be parsed. It can only be performed, received, and entertained. Those who enter this alternative world (that is in performance) find that all the "givens" of the dominant world are simply constructions, and they turn out to be choices we have made that we may un-make and re-make.

By various routes we return from the meeting to our "ordinary" lives as producers and consumers. As we return, however, we have a new narrative identity that need not give in to the anxiety, fear, and dysfunction of the dominant narrative. This counter-narrative, for Christians, is rooted in baptism, but we continue to reperform it at every meeting.

- The Canaanites discovered that they could not keep the Israelite women at the well from singing and dancing.
- The old plantation South discovered that it could not stop Black preachers and Black mamas from telling an alternative transcript that evoked singing and dancing and that in turn evoked the force of dangerous hope.

Dignity, identity, self-respect, and emancipated resolve came out of that singing and dancing.

Such an outcome could and does still happen in church worship. The only requirement is that worship be formed and conducted so as not to be an echo or an endorsement of the dominant narrative, for then it is an act of domestication that serves the status quo and fails to offer emancipatory energy. Thus, we may imagine people wearied from the world of production and consumption, pausing (for twenty minutes) to say out loud in each other's presence:

> Christ has died: granting Caesar a moment of seeming
> victory;
> Christ is risen: Caesar's death penalty had no staying power;
> God's power for life prevailed;
> Christ will come again:

> *The kingdom of the world has become the kingdom of our Lord and of his Messiah.* (Revelation 11:15)

My dad said, "Drink a rest." That is all he said. In retrospect I see that he meant that the work to be done is important, but it is not finally important; it is penultimate.

Imagine . . . "twenty minutes" and becoming more fully human:

> A subversive story!
> A narrative world that can be received but not parsed or explained!
> Emancipated imagination that will not be administered!

Everything depends on those twenty minutes!

22

THE HARD WORK OF EXCEPTIONALISM

THERE IS NO doubt that "white nationalism" is among the most dangerous and pernicious notions now operative among us. Only the most brazen will use the phrase out loud, but "dog whistles" about it are everywhere . . . the notion that "America" (meaning the "United States") is destined and constituted as a white political community in which all others are unwelcome intruders. Given such a pernicious assumption, all manner of action is legitimated, including white aggressive violence in the service of "freedom." And of course the insidious notion of "replacement" feeds the worst inclinations in this direction.

The notion of US exceptionalism has very old roots. Its classic formulation (with the "white" part only voiced inchoately) is the master work of Cotton Mather in 1702. Mather, a New England pastor-theologian, wrote an interpretive history and anticipation of "America" in which he showed how the European settlement of "the new land" was a replication and reiteration of the old biblical narrative of conquest of the land of Canaan by the Israelites, *Magnalia Christa Americana.* As the Israelites were "chosen" by God to receive the "land of promise," so (white) Europeans were to receive the new "land of promise" by evicting the extant population (Native Americans). This early rendering of US narration thus has biblical roots that lend a dimension of theological legitimacy to the enterprise of "America." A parade of like-minded storytellers has faithfully followed Cotton. Of late the doctrine of white entitlement has become aggressive and now lives at the edge of violence in our political discourse.

The church cannot keep silent in the face of such a pernicious distortion of our biblical tradition. In considering white nationalism, we do well to push back to the biblical claims to which Mather appealed. We will not find "nationalism" in the Bible, because such a phenomenon arose only in modern time in the eighteenth century. The biblical cognate to "nationalism" is "exceptionalism" that asserts that Israel is the "chosen people" summoned to perform God's will in the world and to receive God's blessing of land in and through the historical process. Thus, we do well to consider "chosenness" in the Bible as it reappears in modern phrasing in contemporary nationalism.

My thought is this: It is the work of the church, in its consideration of the biblical tradition, to exhibit the *complex, unsettled, problematic element* of every claim of *election*, *entitlement*, *chosenness*, *exceptionalism*, and *privilege* as it is expressed in our various "isms," notably *racism*, *sexism*, and here especially *nationalism*. The fact that such claims are readily seen as complex, unsettled, and problematic serves to undermine the certitude of such present dangerous posturing.

The biblical rootage for the notion of "chosenness" is twofold. On the one hand, chosenness is as old and deep as the memory of Abraham. Indeed, the biblical narrative gets underway with God's initial summons to Abraham, a summons that can readily be seen as God's decisive response to the failure of "world history" in Genesis 1–11:

> *Now the Lord said to Abram, "Go from your country and your kindred and your father's house to the land that I will show you. I will make of you a great nation, and I will bless you, and make your name great, so that you will be a blessing. I will bless those who bless you, and the one who curses you I will curse, and in you all the families of the earth shall be blessed."* (Genesis 12:1–3)

Two matters stand out in this summons. First, the overriding matter is that Abram is to receive a land. This topic is further clarified in Genesis

15:18–21. Israel's history and destiny are to be on the way to "the land of promise." Second, land promise is in the context of other nations who are to be blessed by and in and through the people of Israel. This twofold accent delicately balances the deep commitment of God to Israel and the insistence that Israel as chosen does not and will not exist in a historical vacuum but must deal constructively with other neighboring peoples.

It is quite remarkable that Abram figures very little in the biblical tradition prior to the exile, so much so that John van Seters (*Abraham in History and Tradition*, 2015) has opined that "Abraham" is a very late emergent in the tradition. However that may be, Abram begins to appear in the exile and post-exile as a grounding for hope; Abram is a carrier of God's good promise in a way that becomes counter to despair over intolerable historical circumstances:

> *But you, Israel, my servant,*
> *Jacob, whom I have chosen,*
> *the offspring of Abraham, my friend;*
> *you whom I took from the ends of the earth,*
> *. . . do not fear, for I am with you,*
> *do not be afraid, for I am your God.*
> (Isaiah 41:8; see 51:2, 63:26, Jeremiah 33:26, Ezekiel 33:24)

With good reason the apostle Paul presents Abraham as the primary carrier of the free grace given by God:

> *those who share the faith of Abraham . . . in presence of the God in whom he believed, who gives life to the dead and calls into existence the things that do not exist.* (Romans 4:16–17)

The other biblical rootage of chosenness is in the exodus event in which God is seen to take a "mixed multitude" (Exodus 12:38) of slaves and calls them to be

> *my treasured possession out of all the peoples: Indeed, the earth is mine, but you shall be for me a priestly kingdom and a holy nation.* (Exodus 19:5–6)

This "chosenness" is Israel's entry into the Sinai covenant and the mandates of Torah. The erstwhile slaves, "nobodies" in the face of history, are reckoned to be God's "firstborn son" (Exodus 4:22), to have the privileges and rights of an heir.

On both counts—concerning Abraham and concerning the people of the exodus—chosenness is a designation of the vulnerable who of themselves can have no leverage or claim on the historical process and can legitimately expect nothing from the historical process. Thus, "chosenness" is a forceful designation that counters the political facts on the ground. It is a lordly act in the face of historical reality, that God's commitment to this nobody-people gives them a viable way to be in the world among the nations. Israel is said to be an exceptional people and this exceptionalism is a counterfactual claim of faith. In both of these traditions, the endgame is the land of promise.

It is to be noted (and is often noted) that unlike the Abraham tradition, the Moses tradition of "chosenness" is premised on the "if" of Torah obedience:

> *Now therefore,* if *you obey my voice and keep my covenant.* (Exodus 19:5)

This conditionality of chosenness becomes a defining mark of Torah teaching in the tradition of Deuteronomy, so much so that everything depends upon willing, complete Torah obedience. This claim of conditionality is what shapes the "sanctions" of covenantal prospects for "blessing or curse" in Deuteronomy 28 that is formulated around the double "if" of verses 1 and 15. This element in the tradition of covenant can eventuate, in the thought and faith of Israel, that

Torah disobedience can indeed lead to Israel's forfeiture of its status as "chosen."

When Israel came to royal power, via David and Solomon, it was easy enough to forget the conditional "if" of chosenness and to assume that chosenness was a guaranteed status without any conditional terms. The claim was grandly voiced in royal liturgies:

> *You said, "I have made a covenant with my chosen one,*
> *I have sworn to my servant David;*
> *'I will establish your descendants forever,*
> *and build your throne for all generations.'"...*
> *I will not remove from him my steadfast love,*
> *or be false to my holiness.*
> *I will not violate my covenant,*
> *or alter the word that went forth from my lips.*
> *Once and for all I have sworn by my holiness;*
> *I will not lie to David.*
> *His line shall continue forever,*
> *and his throne endure before me like the sun.*
> *It shall be established forever like the moon."*
> (Psalm 89:3–4, 33–37)

Thus, the historical movement from *powerlessness* to *power* radically repositioned the claim of chosenness. It is only the lingering insistence of the tradition of Deuteronomy that continues, in unwelcome nagging terms, to remind Israel of the conditionality of its status as chosen:

> *If you will walk in my ways, keeping my statutes and my commandments, as your father David walked, then I will lengthen your life.* (1 Kings 3:14; see 6:11–13, 9:4–9; see also Walter Brueggemann, Solomon: Israel's Ironic Icon of Achievement, 139–159)

Thus, we may see that much of the Old Testament tradition is a contestation between two very different notions of chosenness—*unconditional* and *conditional.* The terms, moreover, take on great force when they are variously voiced in contexts of *power* and *powerlessness.* In its seasons of royal power, Israel can imagine unconditional chosenness. Or in such seasons of power it can notice that conditions are imposed even upon power, because the covenantal insistences of Torah are not voided by power. Conversely, Israel in its seasons of powerlessness can in great hope cling to unconditional covenant, but is much more likely to consider the conditions that must be accepted. The outcome is a rich field of interpretation that invites great contestation among these options.

The prophetic tradition of ancient Israel must come to terms with the claim of chosenness by Israel. We may consider as representative three utterances in Amos. First, in Amos 7, the prophet can envision great threats that endanger Israel. In response to each threat the prophet utters a petition for Israel:

> *O Lord God, forgive, I beg you!*
> *How can Jacob stand?*
> *He is so small!* (7:2; see v. 4)

In both cases God heard the prayer of the prophet and "relents." In the third case, however, there is no such petition or relenting. Thus, the prophet speaks up for the claim of Israel in its acute vulnerability.

Second, in Amos 3:2 the prophet verifies Israel's special claim of chosenness:

> *You only have I known of all the families of the earth.* (3:2)

In this usage "know" affirms chosenness. But then in the very next line, the prophet reverses field with a decisive "therefore" that chosenness brings acute divine judgment:

> *Therefore I will punish you for all your iniquities.*

It is Israel's chosen status that evokes God's punishment!

Third, in 9:7, the prophet utters one of the most remarkable statements about Israel's special status as chosen. He first proposes that Israel is like the Ethiopians, that is, a community of Blacks. This rhetorical question requires an answer of "Yes." Yes, Israel is like Ethiopia. In the second rhetorical question, the prophet states the way in which Israel is like the other nations. It is like the other nations in that all of them, Israel and the others, have received an exodus from God. Yes, God caused exodus for Israel. But yes, God caused an exodus for the Palestinians! And for the Arameans! God caused an exodus for each of Israel's two historical enemies. The verse seems to explode and nullify any claim of exceptionalism. Verse 8 characterizes Israel as a "sinful nation" that will be destroyed. This firm divine resolve is final. Except that it is not! At the end of verse 8, the prophet (or an editor) has added a statement that refuses the preceding:

> Except *that I will not utterly destroy the house of Jacob, says the Lord.* (9:8)

The utterance is without explanation. It is as though at the very last instant God cannot and will not give a final negative verdict concerning Israel. That "except" is perhaps the final inflection of "exceptionalism!" This final line functions to exhibit how unsettled is the claim of chosenness. I suggest that taken together Amos 7:1–6, 3:2, and 9:7–8 indicate how complex and unsettled is the notion of chosenness in Israel. Chosenness is a legitimate claim, says the prophet. But it is a claim that is profoundly vexed and problematic. The matters of *power* and *powerlessness*, of *conditionality* and *unconditionality*, swirl around the claim.

At the end of the prophetic utterance in the Old Testament we may consider one other promissory oracle. In Isaiah 19 the prophet considers the ill-fated future of Egypt, the classic enemy of ancient Israel. But then in a late reprise, the prophet can utter these remarkable words:

> *On that day Israel will be the third with Egypt and Assyria, a blessing in the midst of the earth, whom the Lord of hosts has blessed, saying, "blessed be Egypt my people, Assyria the work of my hands, and Israel my heritage."* (Isaiah 19:24–25)

The prophet has before him a map of the Fertile Crescent that always has powerful Egypt to the south and some powerful force in the north (in this case Assyria), with vulnerable Israel between. But now, in God's good time, the prophet anticipates a reordered world of easy well-being among these three peoples. In a breathtaking utterance, the prophet has God assign three "pet names" for Israel to these erstwhile adversaries of Israel:

> Egypt . . . my people,
> Assyria . . . the work of my hands,
> Israel . . . my heritage.

These are all names for a chosen people, all names used elsewhere for Israel. But now these pet names are redistributed across the map. Israel is now among those treasured by God. All are chosen by God! All peoples, including Israel, are beloved by God! Israel itself has no peculiar claim to being exceptional, except along with the others.

It is my thought that the church and its pastors have work to do to help folk to see the unsettled complexity of the claim of exceptionalism, to see how fraught is the notion of chosenness as it faces questions of power and powerlessness, of conditionality and unconditionality. Very many Americans who have never heard of Cotton

Mather have inhaled his easy equation of the *biblical notion of chosenness* with the *destiny of the United States.* In that reading, exceptionalism is easy and obvious, made even more so when it is recognized that Mather had in mind only white Americans. It was Mather's white European vision of America that provided theological legitimacy for the killing of Native Americans and the enslavement of African Americans. It is the easy assumption that now drives so much energy in our midst toward white supremacy. It is, moreover, the unthinkable thought that white privilege and entitlement are now in jeopardy that evokes violence.

But the Bible knows better than that. The Bible knows that every claim to chosenness brings with it hard questions and leaves open the questioning that admits no "ease in Zion," that is, no ease among the would-be chosen. Given the durable force of Mather's affirmation, we cannot, I believe, simply dismiss the claim of chosenness. But we can help folk to see that the claim is not obvious or simple, uncritical, or without self-serving motives. Well before us Israel had to cope with the unsettled complexity of its defining claim. Our work is to show that the biblical foundation for Mather's ideology is itself deeply problematic in a way that many American Christians do not suspect. But the Bible has affirmed from the outset that God has no easy alliances with any nation-state or any race, including our own. It is astonishing that the God of the Bible, the God of Israel, is alert to the claims of other peoples who can also imagine themselves being chosen. That is why the church sings:

> *This is my song, O God of all the nations,*
> *a song of peace for lands afar and mine.*
> *This is my home, the country where my heart is;*
> *here are my hopes, my dreams, my holy shrine;*
> *but other hearts in other lands are beating*
> *with hopes and dreams as true and high as mine.*

My country's skies are bluer than the ocean,
and sunlight beams on cloverleaf and pine.
But other lands have sunlight too, and clover,
and hearts united learn to live as one.
So hear my song, O God of all nations,
a song of peace for their land and for mine.
(*Glory to God*, 340).

23

THE ETHICAL DIGNITY OF THE OTHER

ENRIQUE DUSSEL, AN Argentinian-Mexican scholar and critical commentator, has published a rich stream of books. Unfortunately, much of his work has not yet been translated into English. One of his books that has been translated into English is *The Invention of the Americas: Eclipse of "the Other" and the Myth of Modernity* (1995). In this book Dussel takes up the crucial critical notion that historical significance and cultural development has its rootage in Europe. The history of the world writ large, moreover, is the slow, deliberate process by which European historical significance and cultural development *flowed to the West*, to Africa, eventually to Asia, and to the "invention of the Americas" as a European project. It was a movement that arrived under the flag of "modernity" whereby Europe imposed its power, order, and interpretive categories on the rest of the world. That imposition was a brutal enterprise. The movement proceeded by:

- *colonialization* that sought the wealth of the world (gold!) to the advantage of Europe,
- *enslavement* as it reduced indigenous populations to the cheapest, most exploitative labor force, and
- *genocide* that was free, with the essential blessing of the church, to eliminate populations that were an impediment to European progress and hegemony.

The conclusion that Dussel draws is that Europeans, in their imposition of intellectual, political, and interpretive categories on the rest of the world, were wholly unappreciative of local, native cultures and learning. That lack of appreciation led to the conclusion that "other peoples" were the unacceptable "other," that is, different in ways that were therefore unfamiliar, unwelcome, and dangerous.

Thus, European modernity had at its rootage the dismissal or elimination of the "other" that did not meet European expectations and requirements. Such dismissal and elimination variously could take the form of colonialism, enslavement, or genocide. Thus, the backside of European Enlightenment rationality is barbarism toward the "other."

Dussel traces the workings of what he terms "the triangle of death" through which *Europeans* produced arms and other tools, exchanged them on *the western coast of Africa* for slaves, and then traded the slaves in the *New World of the Caribbean* for gold, silver, and tropical products. The proceeds of such trade were then deposited "in the banks of London and the pantries of the Low Countries" (123). And then Dussel adds wryly:

> *Thus modernity pursued its civilizing, modernizing, humanizing, Christianizing course.* (123)

After he offers this exposé, Dussel proposes a very different history of the world that began in the Fertile Crescent, moved through Asia and Africa, and came only very late to the West, and thus to Europe. This course of world development was not fixed so grossly on profit, and so is not characterized by the same violence of colonization, enslavement, and genocide. Thus, Dussel insists that the world can be rendered very differently, outside of the controlling categories of European hegemony.

At the end of his book, Dussel reflects on what is required to counter this violent reductive modernity in which the "Invention of the Americas" is embedded. On the one hand, he observes that this European notion of modernity presents a strange contradiction between "rational emancipation" under the force of reason that opens new possibilities for human development. On the other hand, at the same time, it uses its myth of modernity to justify an "irrational praxis of violence" toward the other (136). When the two parts of this contradiction are held together, as they have been in long-running practice, Dussel observes that the essential constitutive features of modernity, including sacrificial violence, "are those of the conquistador" (137). The way to counter this contradiction, Dussel concludes, is to deny the innocence of such predation and to affirm the alterity of "the other":

> *This Other encompasses the peripheral colonial world, the sacrificed Indian, the enslaved black, the oppressed woman, the subjugated child, and the alienated popular culture—all victims of modernity's irrational action in contradiction to its own rational ideal.* (137)

And then Dussel comes to his important affirmative statement:

> *The discovery of the ethical dignity of the Other purifies Enlightenment rationality beyond any Eurocentric or developmentalist communicative reason and certainly beyond purely strategic, instrumental rationality.* (137)

I linger over Dussel's acute analysis and moral urgency because the tale of Western brutality toward the other is not past history. It is current practice among us. The players have somewhat changed, but not very much. Our society continues to license and practice dismissive violence toward the other who shows up among us variously as Blacks, Asians, gays, Muslims, or anyone else who does not fit the claim of white male Western hegemony. It is the "ethical dignity of the other" that is most urgent among us that requires a full recognition that *the other* is indeed *other* for us, but that such difference need not be received as a threat. The most extreme form of other as threat is the ignominious theory "replacement" by the "other" that evokes fear and, soon thereafter, violence. Thus, we face a fearful social context in our recent and present history

- of *colonization* as a form of conquest,
- of *enslavement* as a form of subjugation, and
- of *genocide* as a form of elimination.

It is all contemporary to us! And every component of it is marked by violence!

It is the work of the church to be about the "ethical dignity of the other." To address this task with sustained intentionality, it is acutely necessary that we examine our own history and inheritance. When we do that, we discover that the Bible yields a very *mixed scorecard* on the matter of the "other" and the ethical dignity of the "other."

1. There is a powerful strand of the Bible that is elementally *opposed to the other*. We do well to pay attention to these texts, and not disregard them or explain them away. The "purity laws" in Leviticus and in Deuteronomy 14, for example, aim to protect the covenant community by fending off the participation of the other. In the catalogue of Deuteronomy 23:1–6, the "other" is excluded specifically by identification, including those with "crushed testicles" (likely eunuchs), bastard children, and the Ammonites and Moabites. In these latter cases the reason given for exclusion is a particular historical memory; we may guess, however, that the grounds for exclusion are broader and more complex than the reason given. The identification of historical enemies, moreover, is given severe expression in the case of the Amalekites:

> *Remember what Amalek did to you on your journey out of Egypt, when you were faint and weary, and struck down all who lagged behind you; he did not fear God. Therefore when the Lord your God has given you rest from all your*

> *enemies on every hand, in the land that the Lord your God is giving you as an inheritance to possess, you shall blot out the remembrance of Amalek from under heaven; do not forget.* (Deuteronomy 25:17–19)

The extreme case of exclusion is the reiterated mandate to enact total destruction (*herem*) on Israel's enemies:

> *You shall annihilate them—the Hittites and the Amorites, the Canaanites and the Perizzites, the Hivites and the Jebusites—just as the Lord your God has commanded, so that they may not teach you to do all the abhorrent things that they do for their gods, and you thus sin against the Lord your God.* (Deuteronomy 20:17–18, see Deuteronomy 2:34, 3:6, 7:2, Joshua 2:10, 10:28–40)

The ground for all this exclusionary vigor is the claim that Israel is God's chosen people who can retain and protect their peculiar status as holy only by severe and ruthless action to fend off those who would compromise or intrude upon that singular status. There is no doubt that the severity of these urgings is very much entangled with historical, ideological, and ethnic claims. But the sustenance of the status as holy requires articulation with a singular focus and with a kind of "theological innocence." Thus, the conviction of being God's "chosen people" brings with it the mandate and readiness to perform severe exclusion. These two factors, *chosenness* and *severe exclusion*, come together in Israel's tradition:

> *When the Lord your God brings you into the land that you are about to enter and occupy, and he clears away many nations before you—the Hittites, the Girgashites, the Amorites, the Canaanites, the Perizzites, the Hivites, and the Jebusites, seven nations mightier and more numerous than*

> *you—and when the Lord your God gives them over to you and you defeat them, then you must utterly destroy them . . . For you are a people holy to the Lord your God; the Lord your God has chosen you out of all the peoples of the earth to be his people, his treasured possession.* (Deuteronomy 7:1–2, 6)

There can hardly be any doubt that this ancient ideology of violent exclusion—expressed as enslavement and extermination—provided an ideological prop for the same practices in the modern period as the West, in its "chosenness," performed colonization, enslavement, and genocide on populations that were judged to be less worthy and so readily disposed of.

2. The theme of radical hostility toward the "other" is of course countered in other places in the biblical tradition. It is this alternative trajectory of neighborly generosity to which the church regularly appeals. It does so, moreover, most often in ways that pretend the tradition does not include the more violent strand of ideology. That violent strand is countered by a more generous appeal to live in peace with one's neighbors who are not members of the covenant. Thus, even in the catalogue of Deuteronomy 23 allowance is made for the Edomites and the Egyptians who, after a time, may be accepted into the community (vv. 7–8).

It is perhaps Isaiah 56 that most sweepingly advocates for the welcoming inclusion of the other. This chapter stands at the beginning of a restoration program after the exile (III Isaiah) that voices a vigorous alternative to the exclusionary posture of Ezra. After the initial summons to "justice" (56:1), the text indicates in turn the inclusion of "eunuchs" (vv. 3–5) and "foreigners" (vv. 6–8). The readiness to include "eunuchs" has been taken as a deliberate, intentional refutation of the exclusion in Deuteronomy 23:1 concerning those with "crushed testicles." It is plausible that "eunuchs" refers to those who submitted to castration in order to receive advancement in a foreign court, thus compromising the status of Israel as a "holy people." In this rendering, however, that willing submission to foreign advancement is taken as no barrier to admission to the community of covenant. In like manner, the welcome offered to foreigners flies in the face of "purity" that aims to exclude everyone and anything that is "foreign." Thus, the God attested here is the God who gathers all into the community so that all may participate in worship together through the offering of sacrifices and the offering of prayers:

> *These I will bring to my holy mountain,*
> *and make them joyful in my house of prayer;*
> *their burnt offerings and their sacrifices will be accepted on my altar;*
> *for my house shall be called a house of prayer for all peoples.*
> *Thus says the Lord God,*
> *who gathers the outcast of Israel,*
> *I will gather the others to them besides those already gathered.* (Isaiah 56:7–8)

Isaiah 66:18–21, moreover, envisions a great ingathering of those scattered. In this case, the ingathering concerns "your kindred," that is, Jews. But the vision moves in the direction of radical inclusion.

3. Thus, Isaiah 56 functions as an important articulation of alternative to the exclusiveness of our society. The same move toward inclusion of those who are a "stranger" is a major urging in the tradition. A mandate to welcome the stranger can be traced through the Bible. In the wondrous text of Deuteronomy 10:12–22 the key summons to Israel in the culminating imperative is this:

> *You shall love the stranger,*
> *for you were strangers in the land of Egypt.* (Deuteronomy 10:19)

It cannot be any more direct than that. Love the stranger! Love what is strange! Love what is unlike us! Embrace what is other. The Israelites could remember their own past history as "strangers." And we can recognize in our own context that almost all of us are immigrants from immigrant families. Almost all of us came to this land as outsiders, many without resources. This insistence of Moses is echoed in the singular mandate in Hebrews:

> *Let mutual love continue. Do not neglect to show* hospitality to strangers, *for by doing that some have entertained angels without knowing it.* (Hebrews 13:1–2)

Here the verb is "show." The mandate to "show hospitality" recurs in the ethical mandates of the early church. Thus, a bishop is to be "hospitable" (1 Timothy 3:3, Titus 1:8). But here hospitality is toward "strangers." This text is often taken as an allusion to the narrative of Genesis 18 wherein Abraham and Sarah entertain angels whom they do not recognize, but who bestow on the aged couple a great blessing that gave them a new future. There is a recognition that alternative futures may indeed be given by those who are strangers who must, at first glance, be avoided. But the mandate is obvious. Here there is no fear of the other, only a readiness to receive the stranger who is, every time, a potential gift giver.

4. Perhaps the extreme form of the embrace of the other is found in Galatians 3:28:

> *There is no longer Jew or Greek,*
> *there is no longer slave or free,*
> *there is no longer male and female,*
> *for all are one in Christ Jesus.* (Galatians 3:28)

This text, commonly taken as a baptismal formula, affirms that the transformative Lordship of Jesus Christ will overcome and obliterate all the markers that make one "other." Thus, in Christ the church is able to see, in and through the Lordship of Jesus Christ, that the otherness of the stranger is overcome and not defining.

I am aware that baptism can and has been readily "weaponized" to impose the strict, close governance of the church. But when it is recognized that baptism is not a "church prop" but a means of grace, it can and does permit us to receive the world differently, not as a company of adversaries who act out otherness, but as those who live and love under the leadership of grace.

Thus, we may trace through the Bible these twin trajectories of *exclusionary hostility* toward the stranger and *welcome embrace* of the stranger that may culminate in baptism. This is not, to be sure, an evolutionary scheme as though we were "improving." It is rather a recognition that all these options are on offer to us all the time and throughout the sweep of scripture. We can choose variously, either to *embrace the other* or to exclude the other, hostility or solidarity.

This matter of the "other" is now urgent in our society. We are currently in a season of hostility toward the other, most vigorously expressed in an "ideology of replacement" that sees the other as threat to the purity and priority of whites and, even more, white males. Undoubtedly, the "other" constitutes a major crisis in our society as "people of color" become more expressive among us, as the hegemony of white supremacy is under assault, and as gender options are everywhere available among us. The sum of all of these "otherings" jeopardizes old patterns of control and security. Through the eyes of the gospel, however, these alternative forms of human presence may be seen as gifts of newness to be received with appreciation.

Dussel's writing is so to the point concerning modernity (white Western domination) with its long-running capacity to embrace a ringing notion of freedom and hostility toward the other. This contradiction is the basis of our society. We have for the most part been able to live with this contradiction without paying notice to it. The tension between the *exclusion of the other* and the *embrace of the other* is everywhere present among us. It is present in the biblical text; it is present in our civic community; it is present in the church. No doubt Dussel has it exactly right. It is the ethical dignity of the other on which our future depends. It is important that the church weigh in on this important matter with vigorous articulation as it surfaces among us in so many of our communities. The church's business is exactly the news that God mandates love and welcome toward the other. We have known this since the apostle Paul led the church toward welcome of gentiles. The current "outsiders" who play the role of gentiles are those who are unlike white male Westerners. The missionary work of the church is to summon us to welcome the other. In this work we happily have as allies Jews who, after the manner of Emmanuel Levinas (*Totality and Infinity: An Essay on Exteriority*, 1969), know that it is in the "face of the other" that we receive the ethical truth of our life. Obviously we cannot see into the face of the other unless the other is present to us and we are present to the other. Much of the bickering around Jesus had to do with the face of the other who could evoke fear and hostility but who, with him, rather evoked a welcome expressed as forgiveness, hospitality, and generosity. The alternative history of the world sketched by Dussel is most remarkable. It may turn out that those who have so long been "first" in history and culture turn out to have been the "last."

> We will work with each other, we will work side by side;
> We will work with each other, we will work side by side;
> And we'll guard each one's [man's] dignity and save each
> one's [man's] pride.

24

PROFILES IN COWARDICE

MOST OF US are aware of the book by John F. Kennedy, *Profiles in Courage*. Kennedy wrote the book in 1955 while still a college student. It was a collection of vignettes concerning individuals who acted boldly and bravely for the sake of the common good with a readiness to take risks away from an easier path. Now, I suggest, we are in need of a counter-collection of "profiles in cowardice," an account of individuals who have refused to take risks or to act boldly for the sake of the common good. Just now our common good urgently needs such risk-taking agents to act in the midst of gun violence. An amorphous fear feeds the crowd. In turn the amorphous fear by the crowd feeds the fear of would-be leaders. What we witness, recurringly, are those who play it safe and give in to fear. Just now, with raging gun violence, there is need for courage, but what we see all around is cowardly fear.

I could readily identify two such moments of astonishing courage in the life of ancient Israel. The first case I cite concerns the Israelites in Judges 6–8. The Israelites mightily feared the Midianites, who were predators who seized Israelite produce and so reduced Israel to poverty (Judges 6:3–6). In response to the pressure of the Midianite threat, the Israelites provided for themselves hidden places in mountains, caves, and strongholds (Judges 6:2). More than that, when it came time to the threshing of their grain, they did it covertly "in the winepress" (6:11). The result of such hidden action is that the Israelites had to "eat the dust" of their beating of grain that was normally done in fresh air, but in their fear it was now done in an enclosure. Their air was suffocating!

It is characteristic of the Bible that the God of emancipation intervenes on behalf of Israel to rescue them from the threat that evokes their fear. In this case God dispatched "a prophet" (2:7; that is, an angel in 6:11) to remind Israel of the Exodus and to chide Israel for not heeding the will of the God who emancipated them (6:7–10). The messenger declared that God is among Israel as a "mighty warrior" (v. 12; see Exodus 15:3). In response to this divine rebuke Gideon speaks on behalf of cowardly Israel. He avers that none of these remembered "wondrous deeds" is now operative for desperate Israel, because God has "cast off" Israel. Israel is now on its own without resources, he judges, and cannot cope with the threat of Midian; hence, fear!

In response to that consuming fear, the messenger "commissions" (sends) Gideon as the one who is to deliver Israel from Midian. But the fear continues. Gideon refuses the divine commission as being too small and insignificant against such odds:

> *But sir, how can I deliver Israel? My clan is the weakest in Manasseh, and I am the least in my family."* (6:15)

Gideon receives an assurance of divine accompaniment in response to his abdicating fear (v. 16). That is all he gets. Gideon, in his fear, remains unconvinced. He asks for a sign to confirm the assurance. Even then, however, Gideon is still fearful, and he acts out his new obedience to YHWH in the dark of night:

> *So Gideon took ten of his servants, and did as the Lord had told him; but because he was too afraid of his family and the townspeople to do it by day, he did it by night.* (v. 27)

(For a parallel in cowardice, see Nicodemus in John 3:2.) Note well: Gideon is not here afraid of the Midianites, but of his own people! After the public agitation of his action in destroying the symbols of Baalism, it is reported that

> *The spirit of the Lord took possession of Gideon, and he sounded the trumpet, and the Abiezrites were called out to follow him. He sent messengers throughout all Manasseh, and they too were called out to follow him. He also sent messengers to Asher, Zebulon, and Naphtali, and they went up to meet them.* (6:34–35)

Now beyond his fear, Gideon mobilized his people for risky action. But again, Gideon still hesitates. Once more he asks for a sign. Because a sign had been given to him, he asks now for a reverse sign; first he wanted dew on the fleece with dry ground all around, then dry fleece and dew all around. YHWH goes to great lengths to reassure Gideon. This long, lingering narrative is the slow process by which a cowardly man comes to courage. In this rendering the trigger for Gideon's transformation is the insistent work of YHWH who patiently but finally brings Gideon to bold action. After chapter 6, the narrative unfolds as Gideon acts boldly and at great risk, solely assured by divine accompaniment: "For the Lord and for Gideon!" (7:18). It is the power of God that converts this coward into an agent of courage. And along with a cowardly Gideon, there is cowardly Israel that eventually runs risks on the basis of YHWH's assurance.

In a second case of cowardice, Israel is confronted by the Philistine "giant," Goliath (1 Samuel 17:1–51). In this case the threat of the Philistines is ominously embodied in this one out-of-size warrior:

> *And there came out of the camp of the Philistines a champion named Goliath, of Gath, whose height was six cubits and a span. He had a helmet of bronze on his head, and he was armed with a coat of mail; the weight of the coat was five thousand shekels bronze. He had grieves of bronze on his legs, and a javelin of bronze slung between his shoulders. The shaft of his spear was like a weaver's beam, and his spear's head*

> *weighed six hundred shekels of iron; and his shield-bearer went before him.* (vv. 4–7)

The response of Israel to this bodily threat is not a surprise; they were afraid:

> *When Saul and all Israel heard these words of the Philistine, they were dismayed and greatly afraid.* (v. 11)

With the appearance of David in the narrative, the entire scene of threat and fear must be reiterated. David is a nobody, not unlike Gideon, an eighth son among the children of Jesse. Again, now in the presence of young David, Goliath speaks "the same words as before" (v. 23). Again, Israel responds in fear:

> *And the Israelites, when they saw the man, fled from him and were very much afraid.* (v. 24)

David, in his youthful ambitious innocence, asks questions that evidence his trust in and commitment to YHWH and his own ambition:

> *What shall be done for the man who kills this Philistine, and takes away the reproach from Israel? For who is this uncircumcised Philistine that he should defy the armies of the living God?* (v. 16)

David has no doubt that he is linked to "the living God!"

In this dramatic scene Israel is unchecked in its cowardice. It cannot think of any way to counter this awesome Philistine. It cannot imagine anyone capable of meeting the challenge. In the midst of the fearfulness of his people, David is different; he is unintimidated by the Philistine. He has no doubt of YHWH's rule, or of his own capacity. He answers the cowardice of King Saul:

> *Your servant used to keep sheep for his father; and whenever a lion or a bear came, and took a lamb from the flock, I went after it and struck it down, rescuing the lamb from its mouth; and if it turned against me, I would catch it by the jaw, strike it down and kill it. Your servant has killed both lions and bears; and this uncircumcised Philistine shall be like one of them, since he has defied the armies of the living God . . . The Lord, who saved me from the paw of the lion and from the paw of the bear, will save me from the hand of this Philistine.* (vv. 34–37)

David draws a ready parallel between his previous risks that were successful to the present risk he is prepared and willing to undertake.

King Saul was no doubt relieved to find a man of such courage amid his assemblage of cowards, as he had no alternative for the dangerous task at hand. The king commissions him and seeks to equip him for battle (vv. 37–38). But David refuses such armaments. The Philistine mocks him. But David is unwavering in his confidence, trusting as he does in the "Lord of hosts." He declares to the Philistine:

> *You come to me with sword and spear and javelin; but I come to you in the name of the Lord of hosts, the God of the armies of Israel, whom you have defied. This very day the Lord will deliver you into my hand and I will strike you down and cut off your head, and I will give the dead bodies of the Philistine army this very day to the birds of the air and to the wild animals of the earth, so that all the earth may know that there is a God in Israel, and all this assembly may know that the Lord does not save by sword and spear; for the battle is the Lord's and he will give you into our hand.* (vv. 45–47)

David is thick with Yahwistic grounding. It is his confidence in YHWH (not in himself) that sustains him in the face of his awesome enemy. Given his extended posturing oration, the action is quick and decisive:

> *So David prevailed over the Philistine with a sling and a stone, striking down the Philistine and killing him; there was no sword in David's hand. Then David ran and stood over the Philistine; he grasped his sword, drew it out of its sheath, and killed him; then cut off his head with it.* (vv. 50–51)

Only belatedly, at the close of this "fog of war," does King Saul learn the identity of this savior of Israel (v. 58). All his grand oration turned out to be true. David's work matched his oratorical bravado!

These two narratives concerning Gideon and David have much in common. Both feature a fearful, helpless people. Both celebrate a man of courage who lived beyond the fears of his people. But the difference between the two narratives is also striking. Gideon had to be carefully nurtured out of his cowardice into courage. By contrast, David knew no cowardice from the outset. He is from first to last filled with effective courage. That narrative, of itself, does not tell us why David has courage. We can, however, remember that in the previous chapter we have already been told concerning his anointing:

> *The* spirit of the Lord came mightily *upon David from that day forward.* (1 Samuel 16:13)

The parallel form of the empowerment of Gideon is also striking. It is said, eventually, of Gideon:

> *But* the spirit of the Lord took possession *of Gideon; and he sounded the trumpet.* (Judges 6:34; Here I follow LXX in the verb.)

In both instances it is the empowerment of YHWH's spirit that emboldens their courage for brave, risky action. In the end, it does matter to the narrators that Gideon had to be nurtured and that David was always at the ready. Both men act in courage. Both are mobilized by God's resolve. Both refuse the fear of their people. Both make a decisive difference. Both are remembered for their courage and their risk-taking that change the course of their history.

I was led to this theme as I have watched in dismay the political responses and political posturing after the mass murders in Uvalde, Texas, beginning of course with the governor of Texas, followed by the senator, and then many others. Everyone knows that guns kill people. Everyone knows that there are too many guns. Everyone knows that disaffected young males, at the peak of their testosterone, should not have guns so readily available. Everyone knows that we as a society are out of control with guns and gun violence. Everyone knows, including the governor and the senator, and the many Republicans who continue to prattle about mental illness and arming teachers. Everyone knows that such formulae are simply good-sounding mantras without any serious substance.

So why the denial and the deception? Because these Republicans are as frightened as were the Israelites. They are as frightened as were the Israelites before the Midianites:

> *Thus Israel was greatly impoverished because of Midian; and the Israelites cried out to the Lord for help . . . because he was too afraid of his family and the townspeople to do it by day, he did it by night.* (Judges 6: 6, 27)

They are as frightened as were the Israelites before the Philistine giant:

> *When Saul and all Israel heard these words of the Philistine, they were dismayed and greatly afraid . . . All the Israelites, when they saw the man, fled from him and were very much afraid.* (1 Samuel 17:11, 24)

These cowardly Republicans are as frightened as were the Israelites before their enemies. They are frightened, immobilized, and unable to act as were the ancient Israelites. In this case, as with Gideon, they are frightened of their own political base, so they give in to the fear and settle for the self-denigrating work of denial and deception. As Kevin Cramer, senator from North Dakota, said out loud that if he voted for gun control his voters would "probably" dismiss him from office. Well . . . duh?? What is the point of leadership if it is only cowardly following the frightened masses? I suppose the measure of fear that governs so many of us is the "conspiracy theories" that foolishly imagine that there are secret sinister forces that render us helpless and exposed. Or maybe it is not "secret and sinister," but simply the empowerment of too many people of color. Either way, helplessness and danger are fostered among us in ways that yield self-fulfilling policies. In response to this self-debilitating posture, we need a collection of "profiles in cowardice" that would certainly be a larger, far more extended volume than JFK's *Profiles in Courage.* I have wondered if the word "coward" is etymologically linked to the verb "cowed," as "He was cowed by his base." Maybe not, but it is a thought worth pondering. One could become a *coward* by being *cowed* by one's base!

In our social crisis concerning gun violence and gun control, so far fear prevails. So far, Republican "leaders" refuse to step outside the fear of their base to provide leadership. Those who have the clout to change our social reality lack the courage to do so. That leaves us, for now, in a poor circumstance. We may, however, hope and anticipate otherwise. The reason we may continue to hope is that from time to time a *practicing coward moves into courage.* So it was with Gideon; so it was with David who was never afraid. We never know when God's emancipatory Spirit may evoke new agents of courage who will act against fear and against perceived personal interest for the sake of the common good.

In the famous chapter concerning "by faith" in Hebrews 11, we have a roster of those who have become agents of the common good.

In these "profiles in courage," both Gideon and David made the list, even in the same verse!

> *And what more should I say? For time would fail me to tell of* Gideon, *Barak, Samson, Jephthah, of* David *and Samuel and the prophets.* (v. 32; emphasis added)

This lyrical attestation to them continues with a summary of their brave courage:

> *Who through faith conquered kingdoms, administered justice, obtained promises, shut the mouths of lions, quenched raging fires, escaped the edge of the sword, won strength out of weakness, became mighty in war, put foreign armies to flight. Women received their dead by resurrection. Others were tortured, refusing to accept release, in order to obtain a better resurrection. Others suffered mocking and flogging, and even chains and imprisonment. They were stoned to death, they were sawn in two, they were killed by the sword; they went about in skins of sheep and goats, destitute, persecuted, tormented—of whom the world was not worthy. They wandered in deserts and mountains, and in caves and holes in the ground.* (vv. 33–38)

Gideon and David, in their courage, joined the roster of those who ran great risks for the common good of their people. That is why we may hope and expect. The roster of the courageous continues:

- It is the work of the gospel to empower ordinary individuals to such risks;
- It is the intent of the good news to assign fresh agency to erstwhile cowards.

- It is, derivatively, the work of the church to invite individuals away from complacent followership to risky leadership.

The gospel is the news that the world is not and cannot finally be shut down in fear. It is the Spirit of the creator God who recruits those who are fearful to embrace the "things hoped for," who act in a "conviction of things not seen" (v. 1).

This amazing chapter 11 in Hebrews on "profiles in courage" ends on a sober note:

> *Yet all these, though they were commended for their faith, did not receive what was promised, since God had provided something better so that they would not, apart from us, be made perfect.* (vv. 39–40)

This is an astonishing affirmation. The work of faith is not yet finished. Imagine, the brave work of Gideon and of David is not perfect "apart from us." It depends on "us" to complete the perfection of their brave work. Specifically, in our current circumstance, some who are cowardly may indeed step up to do the right thing, to "make perfect" the work of Gideon and David. Such good work will not be the work of cowards. It may indeed be the work of former cowards who are moved afresh by the spirit of God who leads us out beyond our fear to faithful transformative action.

25

IMAGINE! EXTERMINATORY COLONIALISM AND SLAVE LABOR!

MY EYES GLAZE over when it comes to "theory." I do not know, moreover, anything in particular about critical race theory (CRT). I gather that many other people as well do not know much about it. Indeed, the only ones who seem to know with some certainty about it are its vigorous opponents who delight to come and scream their opposition at local school board meetings, a screaming protest that is based on acres of ignorance and misinformation. Its opponents have reified critical race theory into a "thing," made easier to do by the regular use of capital letters. Their resistance to the "theory," they say, is based on the claim that "CRT" intends to teach our children to "hate America." Well, we might do better to leave behind the capitalization, leave CRT on the university campus where it belongs, lower the temperature, and speak instead of the slow specific alertness required to recover the racist reality of our national culture. At its best, the "theory" is a way of seeing honestly where we have been and how we have become who we are as a nation.

I was thinking about this hoax of a manufactured cultural disagreement over CRT as I read the great book *Bloodlands: Europe between Hitler and Stalin* (2012) by Timothy Snyder. His book is a close historical exposé of the systemic barbaric killing policies of Adolf Hitler and Joseph Stalin that were implemented in the territory between Germany and Russia (Poland, Ukraine) that Snyder terms "the Bloodlands." I have written "Converting Statistics" as a brief response to the massive statistical report Snyder offers on the mass killings. At one point Snyder considers Hitler's eastern policy, which was to create *Lebensraum* for Germans by emptying out the resident population of the Bloodlands. Snyder reports that Heinrich Himmler and Reinhard Heydrich devised a specific plan to create "German utopian farm communities" that would produce a bounty of food for Europe. German settlers would protect and defend Europe clear to the Ural Mountains from Asiatic barbarians. It was an ambitious plan that depended on displacing the current population to make room for German settlers who would soon occupy the entire area. And then Snyder writes these quite extraordinary lines:

> *Colonialization would make of Germany a continental empire fit to rival the United States, another hardy frontier state based upon exterminatory colonialism and slave labor. The East was the Nazi Manifest Destiny. In Hitler's view, "in the East a similar process will repeat itself for a second time as in the case of America." As Hitler imagined the future, Germany would deal with the Slavs much as the North Americans had dealt with the Indians. The Volga River in Russia, he once proclaimed, will be Germany's Mississippi.* (160)

Hitler quite explicitly intended to replicate and reiterate the American process of land occupation, so that America's "manifest destiny" of seizure of the land will have its counterpoint in Germany's manifest destiny in Eastern Europe. Two terms specify the route of population displacement: *Exterminatory Colonialization* and *Slave Labor.*

Without reference to CRT, we may consider the two terms (two strategies) in turn. The first term (and strategy) is "exterminatory colonialism." This enterprise in America witnessed the coming of the colonists to America, featuring the Plymouth Rock landing, the Jamestown settlement, the Massachusetts Bay Colony, and all that came after. Of course the land was already occupied by "Indians." The colonists attempted to live in peace with these native tribes . . . until they didn't. And whenever the colonists "needed" more territory, they no longer lived in peace, but pursued violent policies of displacement, removal, relocation, and extermination. The matter is fully exposited in an honest way by Roxanne Dunbar-Ortiz, *An Indigenous People's History of the United States* (2014). Dunbar-Ortiz narrates both the violence of the settlement and the durable justification of such violence that took on a more-or-less romantic casting:

> *Democracy, equality, and equal rights do not fit well with dominance of one race by another, much less with genocide, settler colonialism, and empire. It was during the 1820s—the beginning of the era of Jacksonian settler democracy—that the unique US origin myth evolved reconciling rhetoric with reality. Novelist James Fenimore Cooper was among its initial scribes.* (103)

It became necessary to create the false narrative that the European colonialists came to an "empty land" that was waiting to be settled, occupied, and organized. The claim of course had to pretend to deny the extant population that was not so easily or readily displaced. The "legal, moral" (illegal, immoral!) ground for the action was to be found in the church's long-standing "Doctrine of Discovery," the claim that European explorers and settlers had "discovered" the new world, and with the discovery had the right to possession, occupation, and ownership:

> *From the mid-fifteenth century to the mid-twentieth century, most of the non-European world was colonized under the Doctrine of Discovery, one of the first principles of international law Christian European monarchies promulgated to legitimize investigating, mapping, and claiming lands belonging to peoples outside Europe.* (199)

While earlier appeal had been made to "the Doctrine," it was finally, in 1823, written by the Court into US law:

> *In 1792, not long after the US founding, Secretary of State Thomas Jefferson claimed that the Doctrine of Discovery developed by European states was international law applicable to the new US government as well. In 1823 the US Supreme Court issued its decision in* Johnson v. McIntosh. *Writing for the majority, Chief Justice John Marshall held that the Doctrine of Discovery had been an established principle of European law and of English law in effect in Britain's North American colonies and was also the law of the United States. The Court defined the exclusive property rights that a European country acquired by dint of discovery: "Discovery gave the government, by whose subjects, or by whose authority, it was made, against all other European governments, which title might be consummated by possession."* (199–200)

The *romantic narratives* of Cooper and the *legal arguments* of the court combine to create a warrant for the savage removal policies of Andrew Jackson in the "relocation" of tribal communities. Thus, Snyder's "exterminatory colonization" is exactly the correct term for the seizure of territory by the Europeans who had all the theological legitimacy for barbarism in the claims of exceptionalism and chosenness. It was this that Hitler proposed to repeat "for a second time as in the conquest of America."

The second term Snyder employs to describe Hitler's eastern policy is more obvious: "slave labor." That also can be readily appropriated from US history. Hitler would simply utilize the Slavic population for required labor. *The 1619 Project* has traced in painful detail the ways in which enslavement of people of color has been the practice from the very onset of European colonization:

> *The laws, known as slave codes, varied from colony to colony, from state to state, and over time. Some prohibited enslaved*

> *people form legally marrying; others prevented them from learning to read or from meeting privately in groups. Enslaved people had no claim to their own children, who could be bought, sold, or traded away from them on auction blocks along with furniture and cattle, or behind storefronts that advertised NEGROES FOR SALE. Enslavers and the courts did not honor kinship ties to mothers, siblings, cousins. In most courts, the enslaved held no legal standing. Enslavers could rape or murder their "property" without legal consequence. In the eyes of the law, enslaved people could own nothing, will nothing, and inherit nothing . . . Slavery was not a* necessary *ingredient for the founders' belief in Republican equality, Morgan writes, but in Virginia and the other Southern colonies, it proved* the *ingredient. It is, therefore, not incidental that ten of this nation's first twelve presidents were enslavers. In fact, some might argue that this nation was founded not as a democracy but as a slavocracy.* (Nikole Hannah-Jones, "Democracy," The 1619 Project 12, 19)

That process of coercive subordination of Black people belongs in the very fabric of US history. It was written into law, justified by the church, reinforced by rogue groups, and constantly reconfirmed by court decisions. The end of slavery in Lincoln's Emancipation Proclamation permitted slavery to morph into a most vicious practice of Jim Crow that has in our time eventuated in mass incarceration and now, currently, into "replacement theory." (There is that word "theory" again!) This sequence of policies and practices are all of a piece, designed to protect white domination and enhance white supremacy that are readily traced back to the earliest white European settlers and colonists. They instilled it deep in our democratic bones!

In the United States as in Hitler's proposed policy, two different initiatives were operative: *extermination* for Native Americans, *enslavement* for Black imports. But it is all of a piece. It is all about white domination that lumps all non-whites together as an unwelcome impediment for a "Christian population." And of course the pressure in the same direction continues with current efforts at voter repression and the preemption of democratic practices and institutions. The United States provided a compelling model for Hitler, Himmler, and Heydrich.

And now, opponents of CRT are the shameless heirs of exterminatory colonialists and slave labor that are kept hidden in the interest of pursuing not only white control but white virtue in that white control. Such opponents prefer that our children remain "innocent" and untroubled by our true past. The "threat" embodied by the presence of people of color is for sure an unbearable "threat" that can only drive us deeper into denial. All of this is evident, made stunningly available to us in Snyder's telling phrase, "exterminatory colonialism and slave labor."

One might ask, given this unambiguous historical reality, what is at stake in all of this for the church? Perhaps it is this. It is our own Holy Book that has provided the model for white supremacy in America and for the barbarism in Hitler's Eastern Europe. It is the Bible that provides the model for *exterminatory colonialism* and *slave labor*. It is the church's work to explicate these texts and to show the ways in which our Holy Book has offered models for the most shame-filled parts of our national history.

The actual historical "conquest" by Israel in the Old Testament is a matter of contestation. What is not a matter of dispute is the narrative rendering of a violent entry into the land. The story goes like this:

> *So Joshua took all the land: the hill country and all the Negeb and all the land of Goshen and the lowland and the Arabah and the hill country of Israel and its lowland, from Mount Halak, which rises toward Seir, as far as Baalgad in the valley of Lebanon below Mount Hermon. He took all their kings, struck them down, and put them to death.*

> *Joshua made war a long time with all those kings. There was not a town that made peace with the Israelites, except the Hivites, the inhabitants of Gibeon; all were taken in battle. For it was the Lord's doing to harden their hearts so that they would come against Israel in battle, in order that they might be utterly destroyed, and might receive no mercy, but be exterminated, just as the Lord had commanded Moses.* (Joshua 11:16–20)

Note the final term, "exterminated." And just to underscore the matter, we are offered a detailed list of the conquests:

> *The following are the kings of the land whom Joshua and the Israelites defeated on the west side of the Jordan . . .*

The king of Jericho	*one*
The king of Ai, which is next to Bethel	*one*
The king of Jerusalem	*one*
The king of Hebron	*one*
The king of Jarmuth	*one*
The king of Lachish	*one*
The king of Eglon	*one*
The king of Gezer	*one*
The king of Debir	*one*
The king of Geder	*one*
The king of Hormah	*one*
The king of Arad	*one*
The king of Libnah	*one*
The king of Adullam	*one*
The king of Makkedah	*one*
The king of Bethel	*one*
The king of Tappauh	*one*
The king of Hepher	*one*

The king of Aphek	*one*
The king of Lasharon	*one*
The king of Madon	*one*
The king of Hazor	*one*
The king of Shimronmeron	*one*
The king of Achshaph	*one*
The king of Taanach	*one*
The king of Megiddo	*one*
The king of Kadesh	*one*
The king of Jokneam in Carmel	*one*
The king of Dor in Naphathdor	*one*
The king of Goiim in Galilee	*one*
The king of Tirzah	*one*

Thirty-one kings in all. (Joshua 12: 7, 9–24)

I have reviewed the entire list in the most tedious way because the makers of the biblical text did not find the recital tedious at all. Rather they took it as a witness to the God of the conquest, as a measure of success and legitimacy in the land. (This is not unlike counting the number of Russian generals killed in Ukraine.) This is a part of the Bible we never read in church. It has been, nonetheless, a narrative operative in the assumptive world of Western expansiveness in the new world. In that ancient life-world, as in the life-world of European Calvinism, as in the life-world of Hitler and Himmler, this narrative has continued its lethal force, all justified by the chosenness of a people and by the God who chooses them.

Concerning Snyder's other term, "slave labor," attention must be paid to its recurrence in the Bible. Israel had been delivered from slavery to freedom, so that the Exodus narrative looms large in Israel's imagination. The Lord of the Exodus is indeed the God of liberation! But real-life economics readily manages to undermine the testimony of the Exodus narrative. We have an extended narrative of Israel's dealings with the Gibeonites (Joshua 9:3–2). The two peoples made a treaty, and then the Gibeonites acted in deception. But because of the extant treaty, Israel did not kill the Gibeonites (as the merited), but instead,

> *They became the hewers of wood and drawers of water for the congregation and for the altar of the Lord, to continue to this day, in the place that he should choose.* (Joshua 9:27)

Israel did not blink at subjecting the Gibeonites to the status of slaves. In the account of the land-taking, moreover, we get scattered acknowledgment of "forced labor" imposed upon other peoples by Israel:

> *They did not, however, drive out the Canaanites who lived in Gezer; so the Canaanites have lived in Ephraim to this day, but they have been made to do forced labor.* (Joshua 16:10)

> *Yet the Manassites could not take possession of those towns; but the Canaanites continued to live in that land. But when the Israelites grew strong, they put the Canaanites to* forced labor, *but did not utterly drive them out.* (Joshua 17:12–13)

> *When Israel grew strong, they put the Canaanites to* forced labor, *but did not in fact drive them out.* (Judges 1:28)

King David, so it seems, institutionalized slavery so that in his quite lean and inchoate government he had a "Secretary of Labor":

> *And Adoniram son of Abda was in charge of the* forced labor. (1 Kings 4:6; see 2 Chronicles 20:24)

By the time of King Solomon, moreover, the claim of the Exodus memory had so receded in Israel that the king was free to make forced labor of other peoples, and of his own people as well:

> *King Solomon conscripted* forced labor *out of all Israel; the levy numbered thirty thousand men . . . This is the account of the* forced labor *that King Solomon conscripted to build the house of the Lord and his own house.* (1 Kings 5:13, 9:15)

It is irrefutable that the European colonialists in America, since 1619, embraced a "biblical model" of subjugation into enslavement that continues to pertain among us in altered form.

I am all for CRT when it is handled by those who have a capacity for judicious work. In the meantime the church has its own important work to do, to help church members (and others) come to terms with the social models in the Bible that continue to have such pernicious force in our society. It would be possible to teach the matter of "exterminatory colonialism and slave labor" as it operates in three dimensions:

- the biblical narrative itself,
- it replication in US history and culture, and
- its intended replication in the Bloodlands (Ukraine and Poland) of Hitler's Germany.

The interlacing of these three episodes is a teachable opportunity, given the current crisis in Ukraine.

In the Bible itself we do not know "the facts on the ground." All we know is the myth-making power that justified land possession. The force of that myth-making continues, and must be knowingly illuminated both in its biblical foundation and in its continuing lethal force. All the favorite mantras of "exceptionalism," "manifest destiny," and "white man's burden" are present from the outset. As Snyder has seen and said so well, such thinking and imagining produces *Bloodlands*. And we are heirs to it, as Bible readers and as US citizens. It will not do, in our willful innocence, to pretend otherwise. There is huge teaching and interpretative work to be done. It is teaching and interpretation that has immense political implications and that must, sooner or later, end in a national repentance. Imagine! Imagine a world of slavery and extermination grounded in our Holy Book! Only by facing that will we become capable of a very different imagination—the one about "liberty and justice for all."

CONCLUSION

The Wonder of Emancipation

CONRAD KANAGY HAS shrewdly organized the several pieces in this book around the theme of "freedom." I think that is just right, and I thank him. It is ongoing work to make the case that "freedom" is the core theme of the Bible, even though freedom in the Bible is cast in terms of covenantal fidelity and not in terms of the radical autonomy of the Enlightenment. The theme of freedom is central in the Exodus narrative, wherein the wondrous work of the creator God is the emancipation of the Hebrew enslaved people from the bondage of Pharaoh. The core imperative of the Exodus narrative concerning primarily freedom is put in stark terse terms:

> *Let my people go.* (Exodus 5:1)

The creator God speaks an imperative of freedom and intends mighty Pharaoh to obey.

There is, moreover, a direct line that runs from the *Mosaic mandate* to the *evangelical assertion* of the apostle Paul:

> *For freedom Christ has set us free. Stand firm, therefore, and do not submit again to a yoke of slavery.* (Galatians 5:1)

(Nice that we may go from 5:1 in Exodus to 5:1 in Galatians)! The "yoke of slavery" is the way of the world wherein those with power and wealth characteristically reduce the vulnerable to obligation, debt, and eventually slavery. It is the way of the world. The God of Israel—the God of the gospel—presides over an alternative history of emancipation that places us, explicitly, in a contradiction between *the way of the world* and *the way of the gospel.* The linkage from Moses to Paul becomes even more poignant when we follow the remarkable scholarship of Brigitte Kahl, *Galatians Re-Imagined: Reading with the Eyes of the Vanquished* (2010), who sees that "the law" to which Paul is opposed is not the Jewish Torah, but rather the law of the Roman Empire:

> *Paul's entire argument from Gal. 3:28 through 5:15 is then not simply projecting an otherworldly freedom, but is part of a coded discourse among the enslaved nations about the spirituality and practice of liberation from the Roman "yoke of slavery" (5:1) . . . This suggestion aligns with the argument in previous chapters that the principal antithesis behind Galatians is not Jesus Christ versus the Jewish God but instead the Jewish God-in-Christ versus the divine Caesar, the supreme idol of Paul's world. The law and religion that Paul primarily criticizes are the law and religion not of Judaism but of the Roman Empire.* (256–257)

This perception of the Roman Empire is, in substance, an echo and reiteration of the law of Pharaoh: "Produce more, claim nothing!" Thus, the God of the Bible stands as the great subversive of the characteristic ways of power and money in the world.

Concerning the *emancipation of God*: The God of the Bible is of course free. In the long history of religion, however, God has been variously tamed, domesticated, or trapped in different forms of idolatry. Thus, the Psalmist readily attests the freedom of God and the impotence of the idols:

> *Our God is in the heavens;*
> *he does whatever he pleases.*
> *Their idols are silver and gold,*

the work of human hands.
They have mouths, but do not speak;
eyes, but do not see.
They have ears, but do not hear;
noses but do not smell.
They have hands, but do not feel;
feet, but do not walk;
they make no sound in their throats. (Psalm 115:3–7)

The God of the Bible is celebrated as the one who *can do whatever he pleases*, including overthrowing the power of Pharaoh, defying the rule of Rome (via Good Friday and Easter), and resisting the several demons that distort God's ordered creation.

It is the work of theology—and more especially the work of our singing and preaching and praying—to attest and affirm the freedom of God. God can indeed be trapped in our reductionist formulations. Among conservatives, God's freedom is reduced to coded and fixed formulation. Among liberals, God's freedom is curtailed by the self-assurance that "God has no hands but our hands." That is why our singing requires daring image and metaphor. That is why our poetic declarations must perforce arise from narrative specificities that defy our conventional explanatory word. It is the hard work of the church, in its faithful worship and in its most imaginative speech, to witness to God who is a foil and contrast to our favorite idolatries. The full face of the freedom of God includes celebrative affirmation of governance of creation, attentiveness to the transformation and wonders in our lived lives, and the defeat of the dread reality of evil and death that are loose among us. Everything is at stake on our witness to the freedom of God, without which we are destined finally to despair or to self-sufficiency.

Concerning the *emancipation of the church*. In our time, as perhaps in every time, the church is variously captured in ideological claims, rote practices, and truncated mission. Such bondage happens when the church becomes an echo of the ideology of dominant culture all around. When the church is domesticated in such a way, it forfeits its true purpose and its defining claims, and settles as a chaplain for dominant social interests. There are many ways in which the church may compromise its dangerous mandate and its subversive claim. The emancipation of the church may variously take the form of a reformation or a revival as it anticipates the rule of the God of Exodus and Easter. Over time, to be sure, the church has indeed lived out its life by its bold preaching, its glad singing, its honest praying, and its risky missional work that may contrast the church with the waywardness of the world. But when the church is safely domesticated into an "acceptable" ideology, then its faithful preaching, singing, praying, and acting strike us as radically forbidding. We know, nonetheless, that the dedicated community of faith is always running risks for the sake of the gospel. Thus, the emancipated slaves found themselves in the wilderness, reliant on manna that they could not themselves produce. And since its earliest days, whenever the church has been faithful it has run up against established authority with its wager upon a different governance and a different ordering of human life. The emancipation of the church is a permit to live out its true identity and vocation, without the hindrance of imposed ideology. In our society, that imposed ideology has too often been the greed of unrestrained capitalism and, in too many cases, the insistences of white supremacy. In other times and places, the imposition may take other forms. Every such imposition prevents the church from its true work, its true faith, and its true joy. Such impositions may be overcome when the church lives out of its genuine identity and vocation.

Concerning the *emancipation of the neighborhood.* Neighborhoods consist in houses, shops, and schools. They also consist in housing regulations, police practices, and bank loan policies. As a result some neighborhoods prosper with lavish resources and generous institutional support. Conversely other neighborhoods suffer from disadvantage and deprivation with scant resources and only coercive government engagement. A consequence of such imposed differentials is that some neighborhoods suffer from being readily "labeled" and are consigned to a certain kind of social performance. The wonder is that neighborhoods have and can be restored and reconstituted from such abusive treatment when neighborly energy and resources are mobilized with resolve and intelligence. Neighborhoods can forego such imposed deprivation and labeling through attentive neighborly practices and investments. The work is to emancipate the neighborhood from such fatedness by taking actions in freedom for the sake of all the neighbors. Such actions depend upon the conviction that the imposed fatedness is not to perpetuity but can be altered in significant and healthy ways. Like every emancipation, this one is demanding and requires great stamina.

It is clear enough that the emancipation of God, the emancipation of the church, and the emancipation of the neighborhood are deeply intermingled and interdependent. In these several pieces I have tried to give voice to the emancipatory potential that is present among us. That emancipatory potential may take many forms. In every case, it is to be recognized that the trigger and impetus for emancipatory action lies in the restless character of God who refuses to be held captive by our preferred ideologies or our cherished idolatries. In his early sermon in Acts, the apostle Peter proclaims the Easter resurrection of Jesus:

> *This man handed over to you according to the definite plan and foreknowledge of God, you crucified and killed by the hands of those outside the law. But God raised him up, having freed him from death, because* it was impossible for him to be held in its power. (Acts 2:23–24)

Death could not hold him! Nor could our preferred ideologies! Nor could our cherished idolatries! He is on the loose with his transformative subversive power. And because he is on the loose, we can see that it is none other than God who has raised him from the dead. Because he is on the loose, the church may expect to be freshly liberated for its proper missional work. And our neighborhoods may yet be rescued and reconstituted. All of this is an act of hope! It is that hope that has propelled what I have written here. It is my hope that my words will be a wee resource in our shared refusal of helplessness and hopelessness that daily grind away at us. The practice of hope is an urgent practice for the mobilization of the power and resolve of the God who does indeed make all things new. Pharaoh no doubt worked overtime to keep the slaves helpless and hopeless. And every replication of Pharaoh who depends upon enslaved labor has done the same. It is the power of the transformative God, the faithful missional witness of the church, and the possibility of the neighborhood that invite to the contrary, filled with hope of a practical, constructive, transformative variety.